UNDERTOW

A CRIME'S STORY

HENRY GRANGER

ISBN 1453816232

Front cover art by Aaron Rossell

Cover graphics by Lesley Van Leeuwen-Vega

Back cover: People's Bank building, *circa* 1933,
photograph courtesy of Loutit District Library

For my Grandparents Granger

Contents

Author's Note

Prologue   1

Chapter One - August 18, 1933   4

Chapter Two - May 26 & 27, 1933   7

Chapter Three - June 2 & 3, 1933   14

Chapter Four - June 7 & 8, 1933   25

Chapter Five - June 16, 1933   35

Chapter Six - June 21 to 29, 1933   47

Chapter Seven - June 30, 1933   60

Chapter Eight - July 4, 1933   77

Chapter Nine - July 5 to 28, 1933   86

Chapter Ten - July 29 & 30, 1933   97

Chapter Eleven - August 12 to 15, 1933   105

Chapter Twelve - August 17, 1933   114

Chapter Thirteen - August 18, 1933   121

Chapter Fourteen - August 18, 1933   133

Chapter Fifteen - August 18, 1933   142

Chapter Sixteen - August 18, 1933   151

Chapter Seventeen - August 18, 1933   160

Chapter Eighteen - August 18 to Dec 6, 1933   165

Chapter Nineteen, Jan 1 to July 16, 1934   174

Chapter Twenty, July 22 & 23, 1934   183

Chapter Twenty One, Feb 15 to July 28, 1934   186

Chapter Twenty Two, July 29 to Sept 25, 1934   195

Chapter Twenty Three, August 18 & 19, 1933   206

Chapter Twenty Four, August 20, 1933   216

Chapter Twenty Five, August 20, 1933   224

Chapter Twenty Six, August 25, 1933   232

Epilogue   238

Acknowledgments   *246*

Glossary   *248*

Bibliography   *249*

Author's Note

This novel is based on events that happened twenty years before I was born. Growing up in Grand Haven, Michigan, I was a rapt audience for every old timer who was willing to tell the story of the day Baby Face Nelson roared into town and robbed the People's Bank.

America's Age of Bank Robbers lasted less than three years. In that short span a handful of flamboyant young thieves enjoyed celebrity status, filled the newspapers and radio waves with heart pounding exploits, and in the end were hunted down like rabid dogs. The most notorious – "Machine Gun" Kelly, "Pretty Boy" Floyd, Alvin "Creepy" Karpis, Bonnie and Clyde, John Dillinger, "Baby Face" Nelson – have a multitude of biographers. As I read the life stories of those hoodlums it occurred to me that in almost every case the writer became unabashedly enamored of his subject. I vowed that would not happen to me. Then, in my mind's eye, I met Ed Bentz.

HG

UNDERTOW

Prologue

The eastern shore of Lake Michigan is lined with giant sand dunes covered in white pine, beech, and oak. The City of Grand Haven is perched on several of those big dunes, with the Grand River making a long curve at the bottom before flowing into Lake Michigan. The street grid of Grand Haven was laid out before the Civil War in deference to the topography of the river and the dunes, instead of in the customary polar pattern of true north and south. Still, locals refer to the main street, Washington, and its parallel brothers Franklin and Columbus, as stretching east-to-west. The cross streets are titled numerically and are identified as going north-to-south.

Grand Haven is a county seat and as such is home to the county courthouse. In the middle of the little city is a "court house square" and over the years a series of courthouse buildings have occupied that ground. During the Depression the sheriff's residence and jail were a stone's throw from the court house. The town's main business district developed along both sides of Washington Street, immediately downhill from the court house square.

In 1933 the People's Savings Bank of Grand Haven – "People's Bank" to the locals – occupied the southeast corner of the intersection of Washington and Third streets. Across Third in the southwest corner was McLellan's five-and-dime. Across Washington in the northeast corner was the First Reformed Church with its clock tower that kept time for all who had business downtown. On the diagonal in the northwest corner was the post office building, and behind it the Carnegie library. Addison's furniture store was adjacent to the bank on Washington.

People's Bank was founded in the decade before the

Great War by a small circle of local businessmen. The bank's

shareholders, directors, and officers were mostly first or second

generation Dutch immigrants. Coming through the Crash more

or less unscathed, the little bank actually made a modest profit

through the first three quarters of 1933. At People's Bank thrift

was not just a virtue to be pursued, it was a deity to be worshiped.

That point of view did not bother the bank's customers, because

in Grand Haven a man was not easily separated from his money.

❦

Chapter One

August 18, 1933

It was the third Friday of August and Master Julian Hatton, age six, was having a most wonderful afternoon. His favorite uncle, Charles "Bud" Leonard, was in town to visit Julian's mother, Charlene, who was Bud's sister. Uncle Bud had suggested that he and Julian have a "manly adventure" and run some errands together downtown. Charlene happily agreed so off they went.

First Julian and Uncle Bud dropped in on Bud's old friend Nat Robbins in the Goodrich steamship office at the bottom of Washington Street. As the grownups talked business,

Julian peered out a window and watched dock hands loading luggage aboard the *SS City of Grand Rapids* for tourists headed to the World's Fair in Chicago. The triple-decker steamship had been recently purchased by Robbins for the express purpose of ferrying Fair visitors to and from Chicago. The Fair was very popular, so business was brisk.

Saying goodbye to Mr. Robbins, Bud and Julian followed their noses uphill to Fortino's fruit company where Uncle Bud bought a bag of shell peanuts fresh from the roaster. Julian loved the way that Uncle Bud could crack open a shell between two fingers without looking. They proceeded up the street, Uncle Bud cracking peanuts and Julian eating them. The next stop was Abigail's shop for ladies, where Bud bought a scarf for Charlene and Julian was the center of attention in his freshly starched shirt and short trousers. The duo then crossed to the other side of Washington because Bud needed to mail some letters at the post office. Uncle Bud told Julian to sit at the top of the front steps and eat his peanuts while Bud stepped into the lobby.

"Don't start a riot while I'm gone, kiddo," said Uncle Bud with a wink, and he ducked inside.

Julian was working away at a particularly stubborn peanut when a big black automobile pulled up to the curb. From his vantage point, Julian could peer into the car and right down at the driver. The driver was slouched behind the wheel and there were no passengers in the car. The man wore a hat pulled down low over his eyes and appeared to be chewing on a matchstick. Every other minute, the man appeared to either wipe his brow or blow his nose, and to Julian's amazement and delight, he noticed that the driver was missing two fingers on his right hand. Eventually, the driver slowly turned his head toward the steps and eyeballed Julian. Julian eyeballed him right back. Suddenly the driver of the black car bolted upright, gunned the motor and sped through the intersection past the bank. The roar of the accelerating motor gave Julian a start and peanuts flew everywhere. The show had begun.

❉

Chapter Two

May 26 & 27, 1933

The big man with the red hair stood on the back porch and waved goodnight to the white-haired man making his way carefully up the hill. "Thanks for the game, Father," he said with a grin.

A young woman's voice from inside called out, "Ed, close the door before every cat and dog in Long Beach sneaks in to track up my kitchen floor."

Taking a last drag on a small cigar and flicking the butt into the darkness, Edward Wilhelm Bentz turned and ducked back into the three bedroom bungalow. He picked up the chess pieces that were sprawled across a game table and put them in a leather bag, then folded the table and leaned it in the corner next to his new bag of Bobby Jones matched golf clubs.

Bentz was almost thirty-nine years old and married to Verna, a petite eighteen- year-old. They had met in Tacoma, Washington, two years earlier when Ed was riding high. Verna had a nose for money and Ed liked to spend it, and they were soon married. Ed Bentz' profession was bank robbery. His career began in the Jazz Age, and Bentz had participated in more than fifty bank jobs, working with various accomplices but rarely with the same ones more than once. In order to keep a low profile, Bentz limited himself to no more than three robberies per year. He thoroughly cased his targets to maximize gain and minimize risk. That systematic approach, plus a knack for bail jumping, had kept Bentz out of jail for any long stretch of time.

In 1930, about a year before meeting Verna, Bentz had been in on a two-million-dollar job in Lincoln, Nebraska. Just last year, he had guided George "Machine Gun" Kelly through a snatch of more than seventy-five thousand dollars from a bank in

Colfax, Washington. After the Colfax job, Verna pleaded with

her husband to "retire" so that they could start a family and live

like regular folks. Retirement had been going just fine – it gave

Bentz plenty of time for his favorite avocations of golf, reading,

photography and coin collecting. He had become a "consultant".

For a modest fee he was willing to advise those still in the game

on how to play it. He would even case potential jobs for other

yeggs. It was easy money, and relatively safe.

Still, every so often Bentz felt the urge to get his hands

dirty. The previous fall he had planned the robbery of a small

bank in Holland, Michigan, and then watched from a park bench

while the heist unfolded. Verna was livid when she found out

about that stunt, at least until Ed presented her with the trapiche

emerald earrings he had purchased with his share of the take.

The Edward Bentzs lived most of the year in Tacoma,

but liked to spend their summers hidden away on the shore of

Lake Michigan. This season they had quietly rented a two story cottage, the "Sleepy Nest", in Long Beach, Indiana. Unlike some of the more well-known crooks of the time, Bentz felt no need for the limelight. In his line of work, notoriety always brought imprisonment or death.

Recently Verna had received the crushing news that she would probably never have children. Father Phillip Coughlan, Ed's chess partner that evening, was trying to find a child for Verna and Ed to adopt. In the meantime, Verna doted on her nieces and nephews, most of whom lived around her home town of Milwaukee.

Next Wednesday was Decoration Day, and tomorrow Ed's younger half-brother Theodore ("Teddy") and his new fiancée would arrive from Vancouver to stay for a few weeks. "That should lift my gal's spirits," thought Bentz as he turned off the first floor lights and headed upstairs to the master bedroom. It was becoming a cold night and he hoped Verna was warming up his side of the covers.

It was a gloriously sunny Saturday afternoon, and the Bentz brothers were on the fourth hole of the Pottawattomie Country Club golf course. Teddy was an avid fisherman who considered golf to be a waste of time, but he always agreed to play because Ed invariably paid for the round, the drinks, and everything else. That morning Ed had even bought Teddy an outrageous tartan cap, "To protect that bald spot." It galled Teddy that he was losing his hair faster than his older brother. Otherwise the half-brothers shared a marked resemblance, though Teddy was an inch taller and ten pounds thinner than his older brother.

Teddy's fiancée Catherine and Verna had packed up blankets, books, and a light lunch and headed for the beach. The women would not be back until suppertime, so the men had the afternoon to themselves.

Ed had an eighty average and was in a good mood because he was leading his brother by four strokes after only three holes. This was Teddy's chance. He looked up from his putt, cleared his throat, and said, "I passed Alvin Karpis on my way in this morning. He waved me over and we had a conversation." Alvin "Creepy" Karpis was a highjacker and kidnapper who ran with the Barker brothers. Karpis was laying low for the summer and had rented a house a stone's throw from Ed and Verna's cottage. "Karpis says he knows a man from the Near West Side who's keen to meet you. He's a mean little runt named Lester Gillis. The newspapers call him George Nelson."

"Why would I want to meet some undersized punk from The Patch?" Ed sighed. "You gonna putt, or not?"

"Gillis is really hot, broke out of Joliet last year. He's been busy since, or so Karpis says, and Gillis claims he can pay good dough for a safe house and advice of the right kind."

The mention of money piqued Ed's interest. "And what's in it for you, Baby Brother?"

"OK, so Karpis said Gillis would cut me in on his next haul if I would just put in a good word with you. Look, I'm not ungrateful, you can have half of my share if you will just talk to him."

"Don't wet yourself, Teddy. If he turns out to be a good customer you can keep your share. Otherwise *you* pay the next time we play a round." Ed stared up at the gulls gliding in lazy circles above his head, then back to his brother. "Have him come to the house next Friday night, alone." Then the elder Bentz pulled his putter from the bag. "If you won't putt, I will." Without even bothering to line up the ball he sank a twenty-footer.

❦

Chapter Three

June 2 & 3, 1933

After doing the supper dishes, Verna walked down the beach to partner with a neighbor lady in a Friday night euchre game. The big lake was starting to warm up and the evening air was a pleasant sixty-four degrees. If the weather was this nice by the first weekend of June, then July should be warm and August a scorcher.

Back at the cottage, Ed was leafing through a copy of Washington Irving's *Sketch Book* that Verna had given him for his birthday. She had noticed the small leather-bound volume at a rummage sale that morning, and immediately knew it would make a fine addition to Ed's antique book collection. He had not yet poured his usual after-dinner whiskey because he did not want to risk spilling anything on his new treasure. Bentz closed the book and looked at the chocolate-brown face of his Louis Erard wristwatch. Teddy was annoyingly late, as usual. Bentz shelved his book and went into the kitchen to find a glass, but was distracted by headlight beams coming down the drive. He opened the breadbox and removed a thirty-eight snub-nose, slipped the little revolver into the pocket of his cardigan, and sat down at the table facing the door.

There was no knock, just a "Howdy, Big Brother, " as Teddy pulled open the screen door and stepped over the threshold with a goofy smile on his face. Behind the younger Bentz, almost motionless in the dark, was a small figure in a newsboy cap.

"Come on in, Lester, the old boy's up from his nap," laughed Teddy.

Two steps in, and Lester Gillis was face-to-face with Ed Bentz for the first time. The twenty-five-year-old Gillis knew he was being sized up, so he remained standing, removed his cap and waited for the older man to speak. Meanwhile, Teddy plopped down in one of the kitchen chairs.

Bentz was looking at a small man, maybe five foot four, one hundred thirty pounds. Gillis had a thick head of wavy blonde hair and almost perfect teeth. He was fair complected with absolutely no hint of a five o'clock shadow. He squinted just a bit, which made Bentz suspect Gillis needed glasses. The little man's eyes were steely grey-blue, with flecks of yellow, "like a wild animal," Ed thought.

"My brother tells me," began Bentz, "that you know Alvin Karpis."

"That's right, Mr. Bentz," Gillis answered. "We met last winter in Reno. Turns out Creepy and I know some of the same people in St. Paul."

"Call me Ed. Teddy tells me you worked for the Touhys."

"Well, not exactly," confessed Gillis. "I just came up in the same neighborhood as some of the Touhy people. But there was a time when I would have jumped at the chance to work for that troupe."

"But now you have your own ideas and your own troupe?"

"Damn straight."

Bentz stood up slowly to emphasize that he towered over the smaller Gillis. He turned to the cupboard and asked "I suppose you want one, Teddy?"

"I would not say no," replied the brother.

"How about you , Lester? I can offer Kentucky moonshine or some Canadian whiskey."

"Nothing for me. My old man drank enough for three men, so I abstain."

Bentz poured two whiskeys, handed one to his brother, and sat down again. Teddy readily accepted his ration with a "Bottoms up." Ed motioned to the remaining chair and Gillis sat down.

Ed took a sip of his whiskey, leaned forward toward Gillis and asked, "So what brings you to Long Beach?"

"I need a safe place for my wife and kids while things come together. Creepy told me you were the king of this hill and could find me something for the summer."

"It'll cost you about five hundred dollars. Got it?"

"Yeah, I got it! You think I would drive all the way out here to waste your time and mine?" Gillis' temper seemed to flare up from nowhere.

"So the little man has a short fuse," thought Bentz. "Not good, not good at all."

Ed was about to get up and say good night when Teddy horned in with, "Lester is good for it, Ed, and he'll make us all a lot of money, I vouch for that!"

The elder Bentz stared silently for a moment at his brother, then shifted his gaze to Gillis, then back again to Teddy. Finally, he sighed and told Gillis, "Come back tomorrow morning at ten and we'll find you a place. Then we'll discuss the rest."

Gillis leaped to his feet, offered his hand and exclaimed, "Big Ed, you'll never regret this!"

Bentz accepted the younger man's hand for a moment, then let go, saying, "Boys, let's wrap this up; Verna will be back from her card game any minute."

Teddy stood up and headed for the door with Lester close behind. As he stepped onto the porch, Gillis looked back with a grin and said, "Better put that thirty-eight away before it tears a hole in your nice sweater."

It had rained during the night so Ed and Lester left light tracks in the dark sand as they walked along the beach. Lester made sure to stay on Ed's landward side so that the two men would be more or less at eye level as they talked. A cold breeze was blowing across the waves from the northwest and the beach was empty.

It had taken less than an hour for Ed to make introductions with the rental agent, for Lester to take a look around the interior of a vacant cottage, and for the deal to be sealed with a handshake and the payment of five hundred dollars. Lester told the agent his name was "Jimmie Williams." No lease was signed because in Long Beach the summer residents did not care to leave a paper trail. The Nelson cottage was only three doors down from the Bentz cottage, which was a bit close for Ed's taste but seemed to please Lester immensely. It was Ed who suggested a stroll down the beach, but it was Lester who started the conversation.

"Ed, I know you're hooked up with the best troupes in the country and I don't expect to run with that crowd. I'm not asking to be let in with them. What I want is your experience."

"In what line?"

"You know damn well," Gillis laughed. "In your line, of course."

"You mean banks?"

"Absolutely."

Bentz stopped, pulled a little cigar out of his jacket pocket, and stared out at the new line of storm clouds forming up over the lake. "Well, to begin with, it takes money to start, at least a thousand. You need to buy vests, Thompsons and plenty of ammo, and a car that can't be traced if you leave it behind." He turned out of the wind and lit his cigar. Gillis said nothing so Bentz continued. "Any dumb farmer can walk into a bank and rob it; the hard part is not getting caught. For that you must pick the right mark, learn everything you can about the jug, and have a foolproof get. Are you up to that?"

"Well," admitted Gillis, "that's why I came to you. If you pick the mark, case the jug and plan the get, I'll pay you an even share."

"Damn right you will. And what about Teddy?" asked Bentz. "How does he get cut in?"

Gillis appeared bemused. "Teddy will be part of the troupe and share like everybody else."

"That will NOT happen!" Bentz growled. "My brother drinks too much, has no stomach for a fight , and is not – shall I say – the most *reliable* of partners. So you keep him on the outside, but he still gets a half share."

Gillis did not enjoy being lectured like a school boy, but he bit his lip. Bentz began walking again. "I have a bank in mind north of here in Michigan. The take should be at least fifty thousand. How does that sound?"

"Sounds great to me" said Gillis, "especially coming from you."

"For my share, I will teach you a system. It needs a six-man troupe: two vault men, two floor men, a watch at the door and a wheel man. Who do you have so far?"

"I plan to use two boys from St. Paul, Tommy Carroll and Chuck Fisher, and a con I met in Chicago, Earl Doyle. Ever hear of them?"

"Doyle, maybe, if he ran with Eddie Green in Kansas City. The rest are nobody to me," said Bentz. "Can they keep their mouths shut and do as they're told?" Bentz had stopped walking and leaned into Gillis' face.

"Not a rat among them," promised Gillis.

"Well, that leaves you two short. I met some young cons in East Chicago that might fill the bill, Homer Van Meter and Johnnie Dillinger. They don't know bupkis about banks, so they should fit right in with your crew."

Gillis cocked his head, looked up at Bentz and said, "No thanks, no strangers."

It started to rain so they turned back for the cottages. "You can buy the vests in Gary, but it will take a trip to Texas to buy the Tommy guns," advised Bentz. "When we get back to the house I'll make some calls."

Gillis whooped like a kid and kicked at a wave.   Bentz threw his cigar butt into the now roiling surf.

Chapter Four

June 7 & 8, 1933

It was almost 5 p.m. when the dark blue Terraplane driven by Gillis, with chubby Chuck Fisher stretched out and snoring in the back seat, growled to a stop outside Leibman's Sporting Goods Store. They had driven thirteen hundred miles in four days, fixed three flat tires, eaten in greasy diners, slept on the ground, and arrived dusty, sore and tired in San Antonio.

"What a shithole," thought Gillis as he shook Fisher awake before climbing out to stretch. The dirt street was more or less deserted except for a large Ford four-door sedan parked alongside the plank sidewalk. Gillis stepped over what appeared to be a pile of horse manure and pushed through the front door of the store, where a bell attached to the frame made a sharp ding. Fisher, as usual, brought up the rear.

A fat man in a sweat-stained shirt was behind the counter speaking in low tones to a customer. The doorbell made the customer turn and face the newcomers. He was a slightly-built fellow about Gillis's height, maybe twenty-five years old, wearing a freshly pressed business suit and vest, white shirt and blue silk tie, with a wide-band hat pushed back over thick brown hair. His eyes matched his hair, and he was fair complected. On the counter was an open cardboard cartridge box stamped "US Army M2". A few brass cartridges were scattered on the glass, with the tip of each bullet painted dull black.

"How do," said the dandy with a squinty smile. Before Gillis could reply the suit turned back to the fat man and said,

"I'll take a thousand rounds, or as many as you got if you're short."

The proprietor grunted but said nothing. The customer pocketed one shell, turned and walked past Gillis with a slight limp. "See you in the morning, Hymie," he drawled as he pulled the door open and left.

"What can I do for you boys?" asked Hymie Leibman as he gathered up the cartridges from the counter.

"We're here to pick up merchandise for Ed Bentz," Gillis replied. "He called you a few days ago."

"True and true," said the fat man. "Did you bring six hundred?"

"We were told five hundred, " growled Fisher, who now was fully awake.

"Well, I presume you want bullets for your heaters, and them's extra." The corpulent proprietor turned his head and spat into a bucket hidden behind the counter. "Besides, everybody knows my prices are more than fair . . ."

Impatient as usual, Gillis patted his wallet and announced, "I got the dough right here; let's see the Tommys."

"Not now, Junior," sighed Hymie. "You get your try-outs tomorrow, and that's when you pay for the merchandise. Do yourselves a favor and buy a meal and some friendly companionship at Miss Mabel's on Market Street. Tomorrow at 11a.m. meet me at the old Jedele farm outside of town. Mabel's girls can tell you how to find the place." Leibman winced and farted to announce the conversation was over.

Gillis had his first good night's sleep in days because Fisher and his great snore had spent the night with one of Mabel's girls. She was a skinny Mexican gal who arose in time to join them for breakfast and chattered on like a crow, which the usually dour Fisher found highly amusing. That seemed queer to Gillis because he was pretty sure Fisher could not speak a word of Spanish.

By 10:30 they were at the Jedele farm. As they drove up Gillis noticed that the front door of the farmhouse was missing and sparrows were flying in and out. The weeds in the front yard were a foot high. As he steered around the barn, Gillis observed an REO Speed Wagon and a Ford sedan parked out back, and fifty yards beyond those a rusting Case steam tractor.

Fisher offered, "That big sedan was parked outside the gun store yesterday." As they got closer, Gillis recognized Hymie Leibman in a big-brimmed Stetson, and Hymie's customer from the day before. The younger man had his coat off with his shirt sleeves rolled up. A forty-five caliber pistol was tucked into his waistband. He was holding a mean-looking long rifle that was fitted with a large magazine. As Gillis and Fisher rolled to a stop, the man held the big gun to his hip and let loose with a burst of six rounds. The old tractor was his target, and it bucked and whined as pieces of the boiler flew off in big chunks.

"I told you them black tips would cut iron like a hot knife through butter!" laughed Hymie.

"Hot damn," exclaimed the shooter, "you was right and then some!" He attacked the tractor again and emptied his magazine.

"I'll be right with you," Leibman called out to Gillis. "If you help unload this man's purchase it will speed things up." Gillis and Fisher shrugged and lined up at the tailgate of the truck. The shooter joined them and pumped both their hands in thanks. Gillis noticed a tattoo on the shooter's left arm with the letters "EBW" and a heart broken by a dagger. The three men each carried a rifle or several boxes of ammo from the bed of the truck to the trunk of the sedan. Everything bore US Army markings.

"I don't know how you does it, Hymie," said the shooter, "without somebody getting wise."

"Well," replied the fat man, "them soldier boys at Fort Sam must need spending money more than they need BARs."

The tattooed fellow handed a heavy ammo box to Gillis, lowered his voice and said, "Hymie tells me you boys are down here from Chicago to buy Thompsons. Those heaters are fun to shoot and make a lot of noise, but if you shoot full auto they *will* jam on you at the worst possible moment. I say stick with the BAR – fewer rounds but they will tear though a car door like nobody's business." He turned to settle up with Leibman, and Gillis continued trudging toward the sedan.

Gillis had left his hat in his car, and sweat started to sting his eyes. He dropped the ammo into the trunk, wiped his brow, and for the first time noticed a wispy young woman sitting in the front seat of the Ford. She wore a small red hat over a head of strawberry curls, a close fitting red smock, and matching shoes. In her lap was a Big Chief writing tablet and on the seat next to her a Brownie camera. She smiled at Gillis and said with a saucy twang, "Mister, unless you want to burn your baby face you should either wear a big sombrero or stay out of the hot Texas sun!"

Fisher snickered and received a black scowl from Gillis

for his trouble. Gillis glanced back at the freckle faced gal. "I will try," he said sheepishly.

"Honey," the small young woman called out to Hymie's first customer, "we need to get going if I'm going to see Momma by suppertime."

"Sure, Sugar," he hollered back, "be right there."

A moment later 'Honey' hopped to the sedan, jumped behind the wheel, and tickled the blonde until she squealed for him to quit. He then peered up through the passenger side window and said, "You boys remember what I told you about them Thompsons, and best of luck." The Ford roared to life and was off like a shot.

Gillis and Fisher joined Leibman at the truck and were presented with a crate holding two shiny blue M1921 Thompson submachine guns, a sack of square and drum magazines, and ammo boxes filled with several thousand rounds of ammunition. Gillis picked up one of the Thompsons, put the walnut butt of the detachable stock to his right shoulder with the fore grip in his left hand, and was surprised by the light weight of the gun. His hands started to sweat.

Leibman handed a loaded square to Gillis, nodded toward the derelict tractor, and said, "Give 'er a go." Under Leibman's direction Gillis charged the bolt, snapped the clip into the receiver, pointed at the target, took a deep breath and pulled the trigger. With a staccato bark the machine gun immediately spit out a dozen rounds, the empty brass ejecting in a high arc away from the shooter. The barrel seemed to rise of its own accord as slugs slammed into the tractor body, and the last round actually flew over the target. To Gillis's dismay there was no noticeable disintegration of the old tractor.

Assuming a wider stance and drawing down with the fore grip, Gillis pulled the trigger again and a large chunk of the exhaust stack flew away with a satisfying clang. Gillis was breathing very fast now, and felt an unexpected hardness in his crotch. "Ring 'em up sold!" he exclaimed with a crazy-eyed grin.

Payment was tendered, the machine guns were wrapped in blankets and put into the trunk of the Terraplane with the sack of magazines, and the ammo was placed on the floor of the back seat under some bedrolls. Fisher climbed into the driver's seat, motioned toward Gillis and said, "Come on 'baby face', time to go home."

✽

Chapter Five

June 16, 1933

Helen Gillis and her two small children, Ronnie and
Darlene, moved into their Long Beach summer rental the day
Lester left for San Antonio. The Bentz cottage was a short walk
away, and Helen and Verna quickly became friends. Both women
were short, small boned, with dark hair and fair skin. Both spoke
with a girly lilt in Midwestern nasal tones. A stranger might think
they were sisters. Verna soon came to adore the Gillis children,
and they were immediately at ease with her.

After a week, Verna and Helen hatched a plot to take the kids to Chicago for the World's Fair. They told their husbands it would be a great learning experience for the children, but in truth they were dying to see the 'Homes of Tomorrow' exhibit.

Chicago's second World's Fair --the 1933 Century of Progress Exposition – was built on parkland along the shore of Lake Michigan. Architect Daniel Burnham had developed a 'Plan for Chicago' in 1909. The plan called for the construction of a five-island chain along the lakeshore. Only the first island was ever built, and was named Northerly Island. It was a ninety-one acre manmade peninsula, no more than a quarter of a mile wide at any spot, and connected to the mainland by a small isthmus protruding from the campus of the Field Museum and Shedd Aquarium. The Adler Planetarium was built on the northeast corner of the island. The remainder was covered in grasses and stretched south for almost a mile. The surface of the water between the shore and the island took the shape of an elongated figure eight, with the head and foot dubbed the north lagoon and the south lagoon respectively. When promoters of the 1933 Fair looked for a site to house their grand offering, Northerly Island seemed the logical choice.

The 1933 Fair boasted a modern 'Rainbow City'. The exhibition buildings were of simple geometric design, with flat windowless walls and almost no exterior ornamentation. Bright exterior colors and indirect lighting were used to produce a "modern" aesthetic. All in all, the buildings could have jumped from the panels of a *Buck Rogers* comic strip.

Many buildings were devoted to a particular segment of American industry. The Hall of States featured exhibits by which various States of the Union showed off their agricultural and manufacturing prowess. Foreign countries sponsored pavilions to glorify their cultures, past and present.

The mainland arm of the fair stretched for almost three miles along the shore of Lake Michigan, and the 'Homes of Tomorrow' were built at the halfway point. It was quite a hike from the main fair entrance on the north end, so buses were available for the footsore.

The most prominent structures of the Fair were the six-hundred-twenty-eight-foot tall (64 stories) twin towers that supported the 'Sky Ride'. The Sky Ride was a tram system on which a continuous loop of twelve double-decker cable cars carried excited tourists from one tower to the other. Each car could hold 36 passengers and traveled at six miles per hour. Periodically a jet of smoke shot from the tail of the car, to emulate rocket exhaust. The ride was supposed to evoke the feeling of flying.

The west (mainland) tower arose from a stanchion constructed near the south end of Soldier Field, while the east (island) tower rested on a foundation that was across the north lagoon, one thousand eight hundred fifty feet away. Each tower contained four high-speed elevators. Two of the elevators in each tower rose two hundred nineteen feet (23 stories) to the cable car level, while the other two elevators climbed nonstop six hundred feet to the lower of two observation decks. The elevators to the observation decks traveled one-and-a-half times as fast as the elevators to the cable car level, and the trip to the top lasted about one minute. The lower observation deck was enclosed and the higher deck, reachable by a flight of stairs, was open to the weather. The top deck was ringed by a three-foot-high barrier of solid steel panels, along the top of which ran a handrail made of steel pipe. Coin-operated observation binoculars were mounted on a pedestal at each 90 degree turn of the barrier, with an additional viewing pedestal located half-way between the corners. From the top deck the Indiana dunes could be seen with the naked eye. The top deck was off limits to children; pregnant women and visitors who suffered from vertigo were advised to stay on the lower enclosed deck.

A five acre playground for children, the 'Enchanted Island', was located to the south of the east tower, about halfway down the length of the south lagoon and close to public beach and picnic areas. It featured a miniature train with a Boy Scout engineer, a carousel, a theater and marionette show, and a large slide covered by a plaster mountain. Various actors paraded about as giants and fairies. One reporter described the total effect as a "World's Fair for children all in itself. "

The 1933 Fair also offered a Midway filled with exotic acts and popular entertainers. Fan-dancer Sally Rand was a huge, if somewhat scandalous, draw. When Ed asked Verna to bring him a picture postcard of Miss Rand, he received a smack to the back of his head with a damp dishtowel.

It was the early morning of Saturday, June 16, when Verna, Helen and the kids boarded the Interurban for the ride into the city. The Gillis children spent a good portion of the trip playing peek-a-boo with fellow passengers. When that game lost its luster, they stared out the window and watched the scenery change from marshland to small town streets to big city neighborhoods.

Upon entering the fairgrounds near the Field Museum, it became apparent to Verna and Helen that only a small portion of the fair could be explored in one day. After studying the visitors' guide, the two women decided to start with the 'Homes' exhibit while the kids were fresh, take the bus back to the Sky Ride, ride suspended over the north lagoon to the Enchanted Island, and finish with a stroll past the planetarium, aquarium, and Field Museum on the way back to the Interurban.

Ronnie and Darlene were surprisingly good as gold while their mother and "Aunt Verna" ogled the Homes of the Future. They squealed with delight when it was their turn to ride the Sky Ride. The entire Fair and most of the city's skyline were visible to the cable car passengers, and the kids barraged their mother with a hundred questions about the "tiny" buildings and people below. Half way across the lagoon, Helen laughed and told Verna, "I am so happy the kids get to take this ride. Lester is deathly afraid of heights, and if he was here he'd make the children stay on the ground with him. But don't tell my 'tough guy' I let his secret out of the bag!"

The kids wore themselves out at the Enchanted Island. When it was time to start for home, four-year-old Darlene was fading, so Verna picked her up and carried her. Ronnie, who was a year older, held on to his mother's hand and did his best to keep up. It occurred to Helen that the kids should use the public restrooms inside the Hall of the States before hiking all the way back to the Interurban. She turned to Verna and said, "If you'll wait with Ronnie I'll take Darlene to the ladies' first, and then come back out for her brother." Verna nodded her head in agreement and handed the snoozing little girl to Helen. Verna looked down to take Ronnie's hand, but he was gone.

The next two minutes were filled with absolute panic. Helen ran up the beach one way and then back, clutching Darlene and calling out the name of her little boy. Verna dashed into one State exhibit after another, frantically asking if anyone had seen Ronnie. She felt sick to her stomach and thought she might vomit. Then she heard Helen scream.

Rushing back outside, Verna was startled to see a big bay horse stopped in the middle of the crowd. The horse's chest and flanks were covered with wet sand. Sitting tall in the saddle was an attractive, smallish man outfitted in riding boots, jodhpurs, polo shirt and a brand new Panama hat. Ronnie was perched on the front of the saddle, smiling broadly.

Verna stepped forward and took the now crying Darlene from Helen so that the rider could swing Ronnie down to his mother. "'I believe this desperado, " drawled the rider to a quietly sobbing Helen, "belongs to you."

Helen hugged her son tightly, then gathered herself to look up at the man in the Panama hat. "God bless you, sir, for finding my boy!"

"Well ma'am," he confessed, "I may be partly to blame for your little man wanderin' in the first place. When he saw my animal he made a beeline toward us. I had barely scooped him up when I heard your call of distress."

"You are a guardian angel!" proclaimed Verna. "Please tell us your name; I'm sure our husbands will want to send you a reward."

"Melvin Purvis;" the rider admitted with a shy grin, "but there is no call to reward a man for doing his duty." He tipped his hat to the ladies, then turned the big horse and guided it slowly back to the beach.

Ronnie and Darlene were both asleep before the train reached the Gary station. Verna cradled Darlene's head in her lap and slowly stroked the little girl's hair. Ronnie was propped up against Helen and softly snoring. Helen had been unusually quiet since they had left the fairground, and now was silently crying as she stared out the window.

"Honey, it's all right . . . Ronnie is all right, and for the most part we had a marvelous day." Verna spoke in soothing, quiet tones, not wanting to wake the children.

Helen turned to her friend, gave a little sob, and said, "Oh, Verna, I am so tired of being scared all the time! Lester is a good father but I fear his big plans are going to land him, and maybe me, in jail. Then who will look after the children? Not his witch of a mother, if I have any say about it!"

Verna nodded sympathetically but remained silent.

"You and Ed have made it work, and are almost . . ." she stumbled for the right word, " respectable." Helen feared she had crossed a line, but Verna didn't seem angry. "I am beside myself with worry!"

"Helen, I promise Ed will not let Lester do anything crazy. Ed is retired but he still knows his business, and if Lester just pays attention, everything will work out fine for everybody." Verna reached over and gave her friend a reassuring squeeze of the hand. "Hey, I still have two pieces of a Three Musketeers in my purse. Let's you and me eat 'em before the kids wake up and we're forced to share."

They divided the candy and each woman remained in her own thoughts for the rest of the ride back to Michigan City.

❧

Chapter Six

June 21 to 29, 1933

When Lester Gillis returned from Texas with two
Thompsons and enough ammunition to start a small war, Ed
Bentz had to admit that Gillis was not all talk. Bentz made a call,
and on a rainy Wednesday that was no good for golf, Ed and
Lester drove to Gary to buy more necessities.

They ended up at an old warehouse hidden in a service
alley about a mile south of the gigantic open hearth row operated
by United States Steel. The exterior of the windowless building
was coated with the red-orange-black particulate that filled the air

night and day. There was no clue to what lay inside, just a small sign over the front door that read "Parts Shed". Ed parked his big Buick Series Ninety next to the door and Lester followed him inside.

The interior was poorly lit by a few bare ceiling bulbs. A scuffed counter ran from one side of the room to the other. Behind the counter were high shelves filled with what appeared to be random used machine parts. The place generally stank of grease and oil, and the ceiling was dripping in several places. Nobody seemed to be home. There was a pad of paper and a grease pencil on one end of the counter, and bolted to the wall was the delivery end of a pneumatic tube.

Without saying a word, Bentz tore a sheet from the pad, wrote something with the grease pencil, placed the sheet into the message canister and sent it on its way with the push of a red button. Ed tapped his fingers on the counter top, turned and smiled at Lester, then turned back when the missile reappeared with a small swoosh.

Bentz opened the canister and poured a door key into the palm of his hand. "Let's go," he said and in an instant was through the counter gate and striding toward the dark rear wall of the room. Gillis had to run to keep up. Bentz stopped at another solid door which, due to its color and the lack of a ceiling light, was practically invisible from the front of the room. Bentz unlocked the door with the key, the two men stepped through, and the door closed and locked automatically behind them.

It was as if they had stepped into the cave of the forty thieves. The secret room was brightly lit and shelves on the walls were filled with almost every item of interest to the criminal element. To the left were free standing cases filled with revolvers and pistols of every make and model. To the right were gun cabinets filled with shotguns and rifles. In the middle of it all, sitting behind a large Shaw Walker metal desk, was the tiniest old man Lester had ever seen. His features might be described as 'elfin', and his head was topped with three tufts of white hair. There was a rifle bolt in pieces on the desk, which the geezer was examining with a jeweler's loupe. He looked up, recognized Bentz, and leapt to his feet.

"So it IS you Eddie! Hot damn, I thought you was outta the game."

"Mostly, yes," replied Ed, and he engulfed the little man in a great bear hug. When the elf squeaked "Can't breathe," Bentz released him and the fellow collapsed back into his chair. Bentz perched on the edge of the desk and began to explain his visit.

"Mo, this is Lester Gillis. He's an up 'n 'comer who had the good sense to ask for my advice on a business matter. He needs to buy a few things from you." Turning back to Gillis, Bentz continued, "Lester, this is Mo Billings, and he's going to fix you up right."

Gillis held out a hand with a, "Pleased to meet . . ." but stopped in mid-sentence when he was distracted by the reflected light gleaming off a magnificent white, chrome and gold automobile that was parked near the rear wall.

"Never saw anything like that before, I'll wager!" crowed Billings. "1929 Stutz M, best damn car in the world. I keep it inside, away from all the crap in the air courtesy of US Steel." Gillis just whistled.

Maurice "Mo" Billings was seventy years old. He never knew his father, and his mother had supported them by taking in laundry from the well-to-do families of Hartford, Connecticut. One of her customers helped fifteen-year-old Maurice land his first real job at Colt's Manufacturing Company. Billings had a natural talent for fixing mechanical things, and after twenty years of hard work became a master gunsmith. He cared only for his trade and never found time for marriage, children or the other conventions of a 'normal' life. He did have a penchant for fine automobiles, and over the years bought and sold a dozen Stutz machines. After the Great War the Colt company started to diversify away from the design and manufacture of firearms, and Mo found most of the new work extremely boring.

With the advent of Prohibition a demand for gunsmithing grew alongside the black market for booze. So in 1921 Mo packed up his tools and drove west until he reached the shore of Lake Michigan. He wanted his own workshop and the security of anonymity: in the hubbub of Gary he found both.

"Since Big Ed is here, I assume Lester wants to get in the banking business?" Mo inquired.

Ed shrugged and smiled, and Lester blurted, "You bet, and I mean to do it big!"

"How many men?"

"Five, hopefully six," Gillis answered.

"Ain't got Thompsons; as Ed may have told you they're hard to come by right now." Mo looked ashamed of the shortfall in his inventory.

"Our mutual friend in San Antone has already filled that order," explained Bentz. "What Lester still needs are vests, handguns and lots of ammo. If you have license plates that can't be traced he'll take those too. Some gas cans that don't leak. Bandages and sulfa powder also, just to be safe."

Mo was making mental notes as Bentz finished. "OK boys, let's see what we can find."

First they pulled a half dozen vests from the shelves and piled them next to a garage door that was part of the far wall. Each vest was made of thick cotton padding, much like a catcher wears in baseball. Over the breast, stomach and kidneys Mo had added little pockets that buttoned and were filled with thin steel plates. "These will stop double-ought, thirty-two and thirty-eight, and even forty-five ACP if the bastard is not too close. *So don't let him get close!*" Bentz joined in on the last phrase, and Lester presumed it was an inside joke between the older men.

Next, four clean gas cans, assorted license plates and several Navy surplus first aid packs were located and piled alongside the vests.

"The easy part's done," announced Mo. "Now let's pick out your heaters." In the blink of an eye the little man disappeared around the end of a cupboard and reappeared holding a scruffy suitcase. With a flourish he laid open the bag across his desk. Gillis made a small cough of delight. Inside the suitcase were four Colt thirty-eight caliber Super semi-automatic pistols. Each gun had polished bluing on the side rails and a matte finish on the top and along the triggers. The handle grips looked like butternut.

"The frame is your basic Browning 1911, but the chamber takes the thirty-eight Super cartridge. Colt only made a few of these babies, and most were sold to state police departments. They'll make short work of those vests I'm selling you, and from twenty feet away they'll cut through a car door. They don't kick as bad as a forty-five so it's easier to stay on target."

Mo could see that Gillis was about to pass out from pure joy. "Lester, why don't you look 'em over while Ed and I figure up the bill."

Lester did not need to be asked twice, and he immediately forgot about Billings and Bentz as he carefully examined each pistol in turn. Mo motioned to Ed and they strolled over to the Stutz and pretended to talk cars.

"Did you hear about Frank Nash?" Billings asked in a low voice.

"No. What about old Jellybean? Did he finally find a toupee that fit his pointy head?"

"Killed – last weekend." Bentz's eyes narrowed but he said nothing. "Frank was laying low in Hot Springs when two government men caught up to him. They were hauling him back to Leavenworth when somebody opened up on them at the Kansas City train station. Christ, Ed, don't you read the papers?"

"Verna and I are at the cottage, and I only go into town once a week to pick up a paper and smokes."

"Well, it gets worse. Four coppers got it with Frank, including one of Hoover's pups. The shooters used Thompsons. Some of our friends in Chicago say it was a break gone bad, with that asshole Chuck Floyd screwing everything up." Mo kicked at the floor. " I can't stand Floyd and that's why I always make him pay double!"

Bentzs said nothing. Back in the twenties Frank Nash had been a safecracker like Bentzs and the two men had traded 'professional secrets' on more than one occasion. Nash was not one to make enemies. "Why would somebody shoot down old Frank?" he pondered. It made no sense.

Ed squeezed his little friend's shoulder and turned around to see Lester playing 'quick draw' with a pistol stuck in his waistband. Bentzs let out a long sigh.

"You watch yourself around that one," warned Mo, "cuz young and stupid is a dangerous combination!"

"Thanks for the advice, Mo, but I'll be a hundred miles away when Lester makes his play. Besides, if I got back in the game full throttle Verna would kill me!"

"She's a wise woman." They said nothing to each other for a long moment, and then it was back to business. "I have a shorty twelve gauge the runt will like, and some takedown rifles. Bring your car around to the back and we'll load you up."

With a magnifying glass in one big hand and a numismatics handbook in the other, Ed was spending a quiet evening with a 1933 St. Gaudens Double Eagle. President Roosevelt was taking the United States off the gold standard, and the entire 1933 edition of St. Gaudens' beautiful little coin was slated to be pulled from the market and melted down. Brother Teddy had managed to rescue one of the coins from its inglorious fate and bring it to Long Beach.

Teddy was not a capable fellow: he drank too much, could not hold a regular job, and lacked the intestinal fortitude necessary for the outlaw life. But much to Ed's surprise, over the last several years Teddy had become an excellent fence who on a good day could peddle stolen securities for as much as thirty cents on the dollar. That singular talent made Teddy invaluable to a yegg like Ed. Teddy was beholden to Ed for agreeing to shepherd Gillis, so by way of a "thank you", the younger Bentzs had hustled the gold coin for his brother's collection.

Try as he might, Ed could not concentrate on his little treasure. In the week since he and Gillis had returned from Gary, the *News-Dispatch* and the radio had been filled with stories about the killing of Frank Nash. The vultures were calling it the "Kansas City Massacre".

At about the same time that Nash was gunned down in police custody, a brewery tycoon was seized from the streets of St. Paul in broad daylight. He was released a few days later, no worse for wear, after his family paid one hundred thousand dollars to the kidnappers.

These events and others like them were creating a firestorm of rhetoric in Washington, DC. Hoover, his boss Homer Cummings, and even FDR took turns speechifying about the latest scientific methods that would be brought to bear in the "War on Crime". Ed could see a new day dawning for the police, in which they would finally use their brains instead of their fists. "I've picked a good time to hang it up," he thought.

Ed and Verna had shared corned beef and cabbage for supper, and now she seemed to be taking longer than usual to wash up. He stood up from his armchair, stretched, and wandered into the kitchen. Verna was standing at the sink busily scrubbing the top of a glass jar with a sudsy Brillo pad. "Hey babe, what'cha doin'?" growled Bentz as he wrapped his arms around her so she couldn't move. She leaned back and gave him a peck on the chin, then elbowed him to get free.

"I found a box of Mason jars in the cellar and thought I would clean them up for peaches. I want to give some fruit to the neighbor gals at the end of the summer." She went back to her scrubbing, and he picked up a dishtowel to join in.

"This will be our last summer in Long Beach," he told her quietly.

"I know, " she replied.

They washed the rest of the jars in silence.

Chapter Seven

June 30, 1933

Bentz left Long Beach without eating breakfast because he did not want to wake Verna. He left her a note saying he had business in Hammond and would not be home until after dark, and that he was leaving her the Buick and taking the Packard. He was wearing a blue silk shirt and pleated gabardine trousers, but he had laid out a light linen Palm Beach suit and a pair of spit-shined two-tone brogues in the trunk. The dark gray fenders and khaki hood of the little roadster were covered in a light dew. On the front seat he placed a thermos of coffee, a flashlight, some road maps, and two apples. He slid behind the wheel, reached over and locked his thirty-eight snub-nose in the glove box.

With a turn of the key the in-line eight cylinder motor purred to life and Bentzs smoothly backed up the driveway and onto Lakeshore Drive. He cut through the dunes to Highway 12 and headed north into Michigan. By the time he reached Highway 31 it was 6:30 in the morning. Being Friday the traffic was of a commercial nature, trucks mostly. The other cars tended to hold one or two passengers, men on a mission like himself. Bentzs rolled the window down and enjoyed the sting of the early morning air on his face. He ate an apple and tossed the core out the window.

He drove straight through Benton Harbor and South Haven and after two hours stopped in Douglas to fill up the car. Fifteen minutes later, he was through Holland on his way to Grand Haven. A rail line ran parallel to the highway along the east side of the road. Beech, oak and the occasional white pine lined both sides of the road , with a clearing now and then for a small farm. Coming upon a crossing marked "West Olive",

Bentzs made a mental note to stop there on the return trip and look for a spot where men in a hurry could rendezvous without attracting attention.

Bentzs had made good time and by 10 a.m. he was just south of the Grand Haven city limits. He was starting to think about where he could stop to change clothes when a cloud of steam erupted from under the hood of the Packard. The temperature gauge started to rise at an alarming rate, so he pulled off the road and into the driveway of a little farm. 'C Bierman' was painted over the barn door. A stocky woman in a gingham dress emerged from the barn carrying a milk bucket as the disabled sedan rolled to a stop. She gawked at the nattily-dressed stranger emerging from his smoking automobile. He turned to face her with a small wave and a big smile, and she immediately felt at ease.

"Mornin', ma'am," said the big fellow. "I'm having a little trouble with my machine. May I impose for a drink of water while I check her out?" The woman nodded yes and without a word disappeared through the back door of the house. Bentzs opened the hood and immediately discovered the source of his

problem. The main water hose had separated from the radiator

and the hose clip was missing. The woman returned and silently

offered him a large glass of cold water.

"Thank you so much," said Bentzs as he drained the glass

with gusto and handed it back to her with a grin. "Well, it's a fine

day and I'll be able to make my repair as soon as the motor cools

down a bit. Might I bother you for a bit of baling wire?"

"This way," were the woman's first words, and he

followed as she turned and walked into the barn. A bit of digging

around produced a ball of wire and some pliers, which the lady

handed to Bentzs. "My name is Frieda. Please come sit on the

back steps in the shade for a bit."

"Nice to meet you Frieda, I'm Willie." Bentzs often used

this derivation of his middle name as an alias. They sat on the

back stoop and he proceeded to tell her a tall tale of being a

salesman from Indianapolis who was making his first trip to

Grand Haven to call on potential customers. In return she

shared stories about her children and neighbors, and readily answered his casual questions about where a man might buy some lunch and rent a room in Grand Haven, or cash a check if need be. She happily discovered that 'Willie' shared her passion for reading, and she carefully explained how to find the town library.

After a half hour went by, Bentzs rose to make his repairs while Frieda went inside. He stripped off his silk shirt and in a few minutes had the hose back in place. He went to the back door and asked Frieda if he could have some soap and water to wash up. She motioned him inside where he discovered a pan of hot water, soap and a fresh towel. Frieda had also made him a plate of fried egg sandwiches and pickled beets. After the meal Bentzs donned a fresh shirt and tie and his double-breasted suit. He tried to make Frieda accept a dollar for the baling wire and the lunch but she would not hear of it. He gave her a hearty handshake, she gave him a shy smile, and he was off.

"The old gal was straight with me," thought Bentzs as he motored across the city limits. Just as Frieda had explained, the east-west streets were named after famous men from American history such as Franklin, Washington, and Columbus. When he reached what appeared to be an employees' gymnasium for the Eagle Ottawa Leather Company, Highway 31 made an abrupt turn to the west and became Fulton Street. Continuing down Fulton, Bentzs zipped past several factories, the Fulton House Tavern, and a number of celery fields. Just beyond St. Patrick's Church the street turned slightly to the northwest and the cross streets began to bear numerical names in descending order: Seventh, Sixth, Fifth and so on. Straight ahead Bentzs observed a large smoke stack jutting into the air at what appeared to be the west end of Fulton. He slowed his car and turned left onto Third Street. A block ahead on the right, just as Frieda had described, was the library. Bentzs parked at the curb, removed his jacket, donned his hat and ambled up the steps, under the small columned portico, and through the front door.

The library, like many across the Midwest, was built with a gift from the Carnegie Foundation. That Friday afternoon it sheltered only three persons, one of whom was the librarian,

Helen DeYoung. Helen was a spinster and the same age as Ed

Bentz. Still, she blushed like a school girl when Bentz appeared

at her desk grinning, doffed his hat, bent down and quipped,

"Good afternoon, young lady!"

With a mock frown Helen replied, "Please sir, lower

your voice so as not to bother the other patrons. How may I

help you?"

"Well," Bentzs gave her a small wink, "I would like to

buy you a cool drink after the library closes, but unfortunately I

am here on business." Helen let go a shy smile and Bentzs knew

he had her.

He proceeded to spin a story he'd used before.

"Wilhelm Richards is the name my Ma gave me, but you can call

me Willie." Ed's grin widened. "Drove up last night from Fort

Wayne. My boss wants me to find warehouse space along the

lakeshore. I think Grand Haven's just the ticket."

Helen nodded in eager agreement, so Bentzs continued.

"Before the day is out I gotta secure a lease, find a local business agent, and open a bank account. By any chance do you have a businessman's index of the local banks?"

Without saying a word, Helen briefly disappeared and then returned triumphant with a copy of *Polk's Bank Directory* under her arm. She sat Bentzs down at an empty table, brought him paper and a pencil, and told him, "You just come find me if you have any questions, any questions at all!" He proffered his profound thanks and started in to make some notes.

Ed learned that Grand Haven had two banks, the State Bank around the corner from the library and the People's Bank across the street. Bentzs made a list of the names of the officers and key employees of each institution. It appeared that the State Bank was the more established operation, so he would go there first. He returned the directory to Helen's desk, patted her hand good bye, and left.

It took Benz less than three minutes to retrieve his coat from the car and stroll past the post office on the corner and up to the Grand Haven State Bank. Two-story Doric columns framed the front doors, through which a fairly steady stream of customers was coming and going. Bentzs slowly walked inside and was impressed by the high-end Duncan Phyfe style furnishings. He was even more impressed with the heavily-armed guard who was perched in a guard cage on the end of the teller counter. The guard fixed his gaze on the nattily-dressed big man, so Bentzs asked the nearest teller to make change for a twenty and beat a hasty retreat with his head down.

Instead of immediately returning to his car, Bentzs walked west for a half block and entered Hostetter's News and Cigars. He bought three petit coronas, a Grand Haven street map, and a copy of *Harper's Bazaar* for Verna. After Ed was convinced that no one had followed him out of the State Bank, he strode back to the post office and climbed up its broad steps and through the front door that emptied into the lobby. After purchasing stamps and several post cards, Bentzs stood at a customer service table where he pretended to write while watching customers come and go at the People's Bank across the street. He stared at his handwritten list of the People's Bank key employees until they were well set in his memory. After about ten minutes Bentzs placed a stamp on one of the blank post cards, dropped it in the

mail slot, exited the front door and started across the street.

The People's Savings Bank building was a freestanding

two-story building that had been erected in 1910 on the southeast

corner of the intersection of Washington and Third Streets. The

front of the building, being thirty-six feet wide, faced

Washington. The side of the building ran seventy-two feet down

Third. The roof was flat with an Italianate cornice. The exterior

walls were completely sheathed in Indiana limestone and all

exterior elements were made of the same material. Bentzs

decided that but for the rows of windows on the ground and

second floors, the bank resembled a large mausoleum. That

thought made him slightly uneasy.

The main door faced Washington and was recessed

slightly from the front of the building. Two large Ionic columns

supported an entablature upon which the words "People's

Savings Bank" were carved in relief. The front door was framed

by smaller Ionic columns in half relief, made to look as if they supported the large arch above the door. The keystone was shaped like a torch. The front door had no steps, being set at sidewalk level. Bentzs was pleased to see that the only other exterior door was on Third Street, at the southwest corner of the building. Behind the bank was an alley and a mowed lot with some shrubbery.

The exterior walls were lined with sixteen horizontal bands of stone. Each of the four main corners featured a banded pilaster, and there were two additional pilasters at geometric intervals along the side of the building. Each pilaster was topped with a large Corinthian capital. On the second story three large windows faced Washington and five faced Third. On the ground floor two large windows flanked each side of the front door, and along Third each of the five second-story windows had a twin directly beneath on the ground floor. The right and left side second-story windows that faced Washington were of the standard double-hung variety. Every other window on ground and second floors, except for the half-circle glass above the front door, contained a large fixed pane topped with a decorative horizontal pane of leaded glass. So, no person on the first floor could escape through an open window.

When entering through the front, Bentzs had to push open a swinging door, walk through a small vestibule, and push through a second swinging door that opened into a main room. The ceiling of that main room was twelve feet high and lit with a half-dozen ornate light fixtures that hung from the cciling by chains. Several pieces of unmatched furniture were scattered around the room for customers, but the accouterments were not as plush as those in the State Bank up the street.

The floor was grey-blue terrazzo and all of the walls were covered in white Canadian marble up to what would be considered a standard wainscoting height. Immediately to the right of the vestibule was the corner office of the cashier, emblazoned "F.C. Bolt". The office was empty.

Starting outside Bolt's office door and continuing down the length of the room was a freestanding wall that contained four teller windows. The first window, immediately adjacent to Bolt's corner office and unmanned at the moment, was for bond transactions. At that window customers could buy bonds and redeem coupons. The freestanding wall then made an abrupt ninety-degree turn toward the middle of the room, turned again on a radius and continued parallel to the west exterior wall. On the radius was the cashier's window where customers could obtain change and cash checks. The freestanding wall contained two more windows, one for the savings teller and a fourth station that Bentzs assumed was for night deposits and other commercial transactions. All four teller windows were at waist height.

The upper third of the freestanding wall was comprised of a continuous row of vertical metal bars, with a bar centered every three inches. Each bar started at counter height and stretched upward to a large crown molding made of dark wood. All of the teller cages were backlit by exterior windows spaced along the west side of the bank, but each of those windows was trimmed in curtains that could be drawn shut. A hallway started just beyond the last teller window and, Bentzs presumed, continued to the rear door that exited onto Third.

A skinny, tall man with a moustache and an unruly mop of dark hair, perhaps thirty years of age, manned the cashier's window. Bentzs presented the man with a fifty-dollar bill and asked for change in assorted fives and ones, and three dollars in quarters. The fellow took his time counting out the change, pushed it across the counter and said with a goofy grin, "Here you go, sir."

Bentzs murmured, "Thanks," and stepped back as if to make room for other customers while he counted his change. Ed took that opportunity to scan the other teller stations and the vault.

A young woman was helping an older customer at the savings window. A handsome, athletic-looking young fellow was behind the commercial window reading what appeared to be the sports page of the local newspaper. Across the rear of the main room was a seven-foot-high stockade fence of steel bars that was painted to mimic ornamental wrought iron. Bentzs knew that the passage door through the stockade would be locked to discourage creepers.

Behind that fence, situated squarely on the middle of the south wall and topped with a large ornamental clock, was the vault. The vault door was propped wide open and the interior safety deposit boxes were visible. Without even getting close Ed could tell that the door was a time-locked model made by the Donnell Safe Company of Chicago. The heavy steel door was three feet wide, seven feet tall and swung on two huge hinges, each one the length of a loaf of bread.

Even though the outside of the door was not visible Bentzs knew that there was a primary and backup dial to work the tumbler, and a wheel the size of a big dinner plate that would be turned in a clockwise motion to retract the two steel pins that kept the door tightly locked. Each lock pin was made of hardened steel two inches in diameter. Bentzs had learned from experience that the best way to open a Donnell door was to put a pistol against the cashier's temple and tell him to make magic. It never failed.

At that moment two fellows emerged from the vault, an elderly man carrying a paper sack and a solid-looking man, perhaps thirty-five to forty years old, wearing a very conservative vest and tie. "Thanks, Ted, and tell your dad hello for me," the old man called over his shoulder as he passed Bentzs. The man identified as 'Ted' said something to the young man at the commercial window and the sports page disappeared under the counter.

"Well, 'Ted' must be the boss," Benz concluded. All in all, Ed was very pleased with the setup, especially the absence of a bank guard. He pocketed his change and meandered back out the front door.

Bentzs quickly crossed Washington and climbed into his car. He spent the next hour driving up and down the streets of Grand Haven, making notes on the street map as he went. He located the police station in City Hall and the sheriff's residence next to the courthouse, both of which were less than two blocks from People's Bank, and made note of the automobiles being used for patrol and pursuit. He confirmed the most direct routes back to Highway 31, which seemed to be either Franklin or Lafayette. Finally, Bentzs returned to park at the curb next to the post office. From that vantage point, he observed how customers and employees exited the bank at closing time.

By four o'clock Ed was on his way back to Long Beach. He made a short stop in West Olive and was home in time for a late supper with Verna and to catch Jack Benny on the Philco. Bentzs had his last smoke of the day out on the porch, and with a contented whistle went inside to bed.

❧

Chapter Eight

July 4, 1933

Lakeshore Drive was a narrow dirt road that snaked its way north and east from Michigan City along the bottom of the great barrier dunes that stood sentry at the shore of Lake Michigan. As the road reached the resort community of Long Beach there appeared a line of summer cottages built next to the water and mostly below the grade of the road.

Sleepy Nest, and the cottage rented by the Gillises several doors down, were of this variety. Both cottages were square with big double hung windows on all sides, covered in clapboard and

split shakes, with an open porch at the rear facing the street and a
screened-in porch on the front facing the water. The places were
not insulated against cold weather, so they were boarded up
between October 1 and April 1.

Immense wooded dunes rose abruptly from the other
side of the road like small mountains. Weaving between the
peaks was a labyrinth of private streets. Those streets were lined
with more luxurious summer residences and some year round
homes. The residents of the tight hollows enjoyed easy access to
the beach by numbered footpaths reserved in the town plat for
that purpose. Forming the eastern boundary of the town were
the links of the Long Beach Country Club.

Alvin Karpis was renting one of the more posh summer
residences from Ed Konvalinka, a Cicero politician and
businessman with connections to the mob. Perched on a street
corner overlooking the lake, 'Belle Casa' resembled a small
Spanish villa sheathed in white stucco and trimmed with a red tile
roof. There was a garage in the basement that was entered by
driving down a ramp at the rear of the home. This convenient

feature allowed contraband to come and go without raising the suspicion of the neighbors.

On this bright Tuesday afternoon, a casual passerby would have thought that Alvin Karpis was hosting a neighborhood picnic. Several long tables had been set up on the well-kept lawn behind the Karpis cottage and trimmed in red, white and blue bunting. A half dozen young women were busily setting places and arranging dishes and platters heaped with fried chicken, sweet-and-sour potatoes, three-bean salad, deviled eggs, Boston baked beans, sauerkraut with Polish sausage, rhubarb sauce, and a large picnic ham. Dessert would be strawberry shortcake with whipped cream. Each table held several pitchers of lemonade and iced tea, and if you cared to look there was bootleg gin in the dining room.

A like number of men were lounging about smoking, telling jokes and teasing the women. For the most part the men folk were dressed in cotton shirts, slacks and caps, but one of the men also wore a full-length chef's apron.

Portly and slouch-shouldered, twenty-four-year-old Chuck Fisher had worked for a short time as a chef, so of course the women put him in charge of carving the ham. Since making the run to San Antonio with Gillis, Fisher had been renting a room above the Willard Café in Michigan City. As Fisher sliced away, the platter was steadied by Fisher's pal, Tommy Caroll.

Tommy was tall, muscular, and square-jawed. His mother had been half Indian and he shared her dark complexion and jet-black hair. Caroll had briefly pursued a boxing career and had the flattened nose to prove it. The thirty-two-year-old Caroll had also done a twenty-one-month stretch in Leavenworth for armed robbery. At the invitation of Gillis, Caroll had driven down from St. Paul to meet Ed Bentz.

Tommy loved the ladies and was keeping company with his latest girlfriend, Jean Delaney. Very blonde and extremely buxom, Jean had turned heads when she donned a backless navy swimsuit before heading across Lakeshore Drive and down to the beach with Verna Bentz and the Gillis children.

Earl Doyle, thirty-five, had just returned from walking up and down the beach with the two Pekingese that belonged to his wife Hazel. Slowed down by stubby legs and a heavy build, the dark-eyed Doyle had a hard time keeping up with the little dogs. Their long coats were a magnet for every thorn and sand burr, and every dead fish on the beach had to be closely inspected. The Doyles had arrived from St. Paul several days earlier and had settled in a cottage near Lester and Helen. Earl spent every night on the back porch with a washtub and a brush as he fought to scrub one wriggling, snuffling, snapping dog and then the other. He tended to be all thumbs, and more often than not ended up getting the worst of things during doggy bath time.

Watching Doyle trudge up the hill behind the now-filthy Pekingese made John Dillinger smile. The thirty-year-old Dillinger had come to Long Beach at Caroll's suggestion, and because Dillinger's girlfriend, Evelyn "Billie" Frenchette, was desperate to spend a few days at the beach. Billie also wanted "Johnnie" to squire her around the World's Fair, and he had promised they would take the train into Chicago for that purpose the very next day. "But after we get back I have some business to take care of in Muncie," Dillinger had told his girl.

Billie was a statuesque brunette with curly brown hair and big brown eyes. That afternoon she was wearing a polka dot dress, sandals and a wide-brimmed sunhat. Billie was devoted to Johnnie and tolerant of his absences so long as he treated her like the Queen of the May when they were together. Other women immediately liked Billie, and that afternoon she was having a grand time sharing girl talk in the kitchen with Helen Gillis, Hazel Doyle, and Teddy's fiancée Catherine.

Charlie "Pretty Boy" Floyd had arrived at the Karpis cottage alone and unexpected an hour or so after the picnic had started. He and Karpis had disappeared inside the garage for almost an hour.

While they were gone, Alvin's teenaged girlfriend Dolores DeLaney, younger sister of Jean, was all laughs and giggles as she helped the slightly older married ladies prepare the meal. With nobody watching, Dillinger patted Dolores on the rear end when she skipped by. She gave him a quick grin but said nothing.

A moment later, Karpis and Floyd walked side by side into the back yard, talking in low tones. It seemed to Dillinger that Floyd was anxious to leave, but Karpis hounded Floyd until he agreed to stay for the meal.

A month earlier, John Dillinger had been a nobody to Lester Gillis. Upon returning from San Antonio, Lester had driven to St. Paul to discuss the Grand Haven job with Caroll and Earl Doyle. It was in St. Paul that Caroll first introduced Gillis to Dillinger, but the two men did not take much notice of each other. Now Dillinger looked across the yard at Gillis, sitting by himself and leafing through a gun catalogue. "What a nasty little peckerwood," thought Dillinger. " Why does Tommy put up with him? Hard to believe ol' Ed Bentzs would waste his time on Gillis." Dillinger could tell that something was up, and he was jealous that nobody had seen fit to clue him in.

Ed Bentzs was reclining in an Adirondack chair that had been pulled into the shade of a large poplar. Bentzs was flanked by his old partner George Kelly, Father Coughlin and Teddy. Kelly, a husky blue-eyed Tennessean, was already a little drunk from the booze he had supplied for the party. George had just finished telling a story at Ed's expense and was laughing loudly at the punch line. Kelly's wife Kathryn stepped up to steady him and whisper into his ear. Kathryn handed her husband a tall glass filled with lemonade, and he surrendered his tumbler of gin and tonic. She was wearing an outlandishly large ring sporting eight round diamonds, which she had proudly shown to the other women while helping in the kitchen.

"I see Kathryn still keeps you on a short leash, George," chuckled Bentzs. That observation made Teddy snort and Coughlin nod his head. "But she certainly has some nice jewelry. Have you been keeping company with oil tycoons and millionaires?"

"Not lately, old man," Kelly shot back, "but I intend to give it a go. How much do I owe for your sage advice?" That made everybody laugh, including Bentzs.

Bentzs' mood abruptly soured as he caught sight of Floyd walking across the yard with Alvin. Ed's eyes narrowed as he removed a small cigar from his shirt pocket. "If I knew for sure that damn Okie shot Frank Nash, I'd rat him out to Hoover myself!"

"Now, now, Ed," admonished Coughlin, "we must remember to offer charity to the uncharitable."

Bentz glanced up at the priest and continued, "As God and Teddy are my witnesses, I have never used physical violence to make my way in the world. But any fool can see that 'Pretty Boy' is an indiscriminate killer. He has put forces in motion that may be the death of us all."

Before Coughlin could reply, Billie called them to the table with a hearty, "Dinner's ready; come and get it!" Children were quickly rounded up, plates were filled, Coughlin offered thanks, and everybody joined in on the "Amen".

❧

Chapter Nine

July 5 to 28, 1933

After the Fourth, things settled into a comfortable summer routine. Dillinger, Karpis, Kelly and Floyd left Long Beach to pursue targets of opportunity in other parts of the country. After taking a two-week trip to visit Mammoth Cave, Teddy and Catherine rented a tourist apartment in Chicago. The big lake warmed up and the days seemed endless. The Gillis, Doyle and Ed Bentz families enjoyed the sun and sand and each other's company. Father Coughlin recommended Ed Bentzs for membership in the Long Beach Country Club, and Ed was soon playing there twice a week with a foursome that included a police chief, an Illinois state senator, and a bookie.

Verna became the ringleader of the wives as she, Helen and Hazel filled their afternoons with cards, shopping or trips to the movies. During one outing they took in Johnnie Weissmuller's *Tarzan, The Ape Man* at the Tivoli Theater in Michigan City. On the way home Helen almost drove off the road when mousy Hazel confessed she was tempted to leave Earl and run off to a jungle hideaway with the sleek and muscular Weissmuller.

Tommy Caroll and Chuck Fisher were infrequent visitors for the remainder of July. They would usually not drive out to Long Beach but would meet with Gillis at the Willard Café. Caroll felt that Ed Bentz "looks down his big nose at small bandits like Chuck an' me" and therefore chose to avoid Bentz whenever possible. Also, having that "white man's priest" Coughlin hanging round the troupe made both Caroll and Fisher nervous. It was also convenient that the café doubled as an unlicensed pawn shop and the owner was always willing to buy

small treasures from Fisher or Caroll so that they had folding

money.

Father Coughlin went about his normal parish duties in

the Chicago suburb of Wilmette, but all of his free time was spent

tending to his extra flock of notorious sheep in Long Beach. He

kept trying to find a child for the Bentzs to adopt. The

"adoption" would need to be of the informal variety because Ed

could not risk giving his true identity to a social worker. In

appreciation of what the whiskey priest was trying to do for them,

Verna and Ed treated him to a show at the Memorial Opera

House in Valparaiso and a late supper afterwards. The movie

actress Beulah Bondi was visiting her home town and had agreed

to perform a one-woman show for the benefit of the local society

for widows and orphans. Miss Bondi's performance was first rate

and she even agreed to mug for Ed's camera after the show.

The trio decided to dine at Horn's Café across the courthouse square from the opera house. The immense white limestone courthouse was illuminated by a circle of floodlights that were kept ablaze all night at taxpayers' expense, and a passerby could not miss the ragged men stretched out and snoring on park benches. A family with four small children was huddled for the night between two towering oak trees at one corner of the manicured lawn. The somber images of the homeless, dirty youngsters stayed with the priest, so he only picked at his food.

"What's the matter, Padre, is the local cuisine not to your liking?" Bentz leaned back in his chair and took a hearty gulp from his glass of iced tea.

"Well, if you must know, I was just thinking about what the cost of this meal could do for Miss Bondi's charity." Coughlin pushed his plate away and stared out the big dining room windows toward the square.

"Hell's bells, Father, those kids are no worse off than me and Teddy at that age! My Pa was killed by a runaway horse when I was twelve, and my Ma managed to raise us kids all on her own." Bentzs lowered his voice and continued. "Verna had no picnic growin' up either. Sure it's hard times for a lot of folks these days, but we made it through hard times and so will they." Ed's usual smile had been replaced by a look of disdain.

"The Father don't mean anything personal, Honey, but it *is* hard to enjoy a night out when those little ones don't have a safe place to sleep because their ma an' pa lost the farm." Verna had a way of gently scolding Ed that never made him angry with her.

"I'm sorry, Bucko, I didn't mean to spoil the party," Coughlin said soothingly, "and I am extremely grateful to you and Verna taking me out for a grand time on the town."

Bentzs was listening with only one ear because now he was staring at a little campfire that was burning across the street. "No apology needed, Father. When a man comes up the hard way he learns to look out for number one, which can make for bad dinner conversation. I'll try to give a damn from now on."

The waiter was surprised that the well dressed couple and their friend did not order dessert. Instead they gathered their coats and quickly walked back through the park towards the opera house and Ed's Buick. Halfway across, one of the ragamuffins came running after a firefly and ran full bore into Bentzs. The collision knocked the little boy backward and onto the seat of his pants. Ed bent down and scooped the child up, dusted him off, and asked, "You okay, little man?" The small boy silently nodded his head "yes" and made a bee line for his mother.

As the woman looked her son over for new cuts and bruises, she noticed something sticking out of his shirt pocket. It was a folded hundred dollar bill. The woman gasped, then turned to call after the big redheaded man and ask if he had dropped some money. By then he and his companions had disappeared in the darkness.

◊ ◊ ◊

Eventually it was time to get back to work. The troupe still had only four members: Gillis, Caroll, Fisher and Doyle. When pressed by Bentzs about the need for two more, Gillis would curse "Klootzak!" and stomp off. Bentzs finally got tired of waiting and decided to begin practice with a short squad.

Firearms practice was the first order of business. Bentzs had learned to shoot hunting rifles and shotguns as a boy, and was trained to use pistols during a short stint in the Canadian Army, so he was the troupe's instructor. In spite of their bravado and criminal records, Gillis, Caroll and Fisher knew very little about guns. Doyle had no experience of any kind with firearms. Teddy, who came along to watch and tease, was afraid of guns and would not even pick one up.

They began with the Thompson. "This trench broom may be the finest weapon ever made for our sort of work," Ed proffered. "It holds a lot of rounds and makes a shit-load of noise. Understand that you *do not* want to shoot anybody; you just want to scare the bejesus out of the locals."

He could see that all eyes were fixed on him, so he continued. "The Thompson is made to rapid fire in bursts of three to five shots. Shoot accordingly and you will have no problem. But if you act like a damn fool and try to empty an entire magazine in one burst, you may have brass hang up in the ejection port. Then you will be screwed. And don't rest your nose behind the rear sight unless you want it broken. If you shoot with the stock removed, keep your elbows in."

With that said, they lined up to take turns. The target was an ancient white pine stump that protruded from the side of a small dune. Lester turned out to be the most adept, so Ed recommended that Gillis carry a Thompson into the bank. "But take the stock off, so you can hide the gun in a duffel or big basket," Bentzs advised.

They moved on to the pistols. No member of the troupe but Caroll could hit the target with any degree of reliability, and Doyle was so fumble-fingered he dropped his gun into the sand when he tried to rack in the first bullet. "Earl, my boy," hooted Teddy, "I think you better stick to a shotgun!"

"That might not be a bad idea, Earl," admitted Gillis. So Doyle was handed an auto-loading Remington twelve gauge. All he had to do was point and shoot, and the middle of the stump disappeared.

After the cheering subsided, Bentzs smiled at Doyle and said, "Earl, looks like you are the shotgunner." Doyle grinned so wide the ends of his Boston Blackie moustache started to curl.

Ed's lectures on the mechanics of bank robbery were delivered inside the Gillis cottage. No drinking was allowed. Helen, who vacated to spend time with Verna, put out cold cuts and fresh bread so Fisher could make sandwiches for the men.

"You've all heard tell of the James boys and the Daltons, and in the movies the bandits always shoot their way clear or die. Well, for the most part that's pure bullshit. A man who robs banks in daylight has always, I repeat *always*, depended on his getaway and not his gun. The old timers did not out-shoot the sheriff, they out-rode him. What you are going to do is not much different." Bentzs took a bite from his sandwich and continued.

"I will personally map the get. When you *finally* find your driver," and here Bentz glared at Gillis, "I will teach him every twist and turn of the road. You will not drive straight back to Long Beach but will come home in a big circle designed by me." Bentzs took a second bite, chewed and swallowed. "Your car needs to be bigger and faster than the heaps driven by small town coppers."

"We gonna take Lester's big Terraplane?" The question came from Doyle, who had raised his hand.

"No – Earl, put your hand down – you will *not* use your own vehicle and you will *not* use a stolen car. You want a car without a history that can be sold without raising suspicion after the job is done."

"I got a friend working on it," said Gillis.

"You will bring extra cans of gas, and medical supplies. When you're on the run you won't have time to stop at a filling station, and if somebody takes a hit you do your best for him in the car but keep going. If something happens to the first car that makes it necessary to steal another, you will have extra plates with you to hang on the second machine. Bring a change of clothes, and don't dress flashy. Any questions so far?"

"Yeah," Caroll piped up. "Where the hell we goin'?"

"North," Bentz replied. "To the land of thick skulls and wooden shoes."

Chapter Ten

July 29 & 30, 1933

Ed proclaimed that he and Verna "needed one summer weekend away from everything and everybody", which meant he wanted Verna all to himself for a change. She mentioned the possibility of bringing the Gillis children with them, but when Ed made a face she let it go. They packed the roadster with a picnic lunch and a change of clothes and were off and running by 9:30 a.m.

The summer sky was filled with big cumulus clouds but Ed decided to "live dangerously" and ride with the top down. He kept the sun out of his eyes with a golf cap, and she wore a multi-colored scarf and a pair of Foster Grants. Ed gave Verna his watch, a little spiral notebook and a pencil, and dictated travel notes to her as they drove along. This was something they had done before, and Verna was getting to be an old hand.

They hit a long straight stretch of road, so Ed began enthusiastically describing his plan to build them a new home in Nevada near the huge reservoir that was being created in Boulder Canyon.

"I want us to grow old in a big Prairie House like the one Frank Lloyd Wright built for himself in Wisconsin."

Verna pretended to pout. "You only want to move west because you love golf more than me." Ed's rejoinder was to reach out a big paw, pull her tight to him, and kiss her sloppily on the top of the head. Verna beamed.

After crossing into Michigan the Bentz traveled east and north through Niles, Dowagiac and Paw Paw before stopping in Allegan to eat lunch. Ed parked the car and Verna unfolded a blanket on the banks of a little river that bisected the town. In front of them was a small dam and millpond, and Verna fed the remains of her lunch to a mother duck and six ducklings while Ed snapped still photos with his Ansco and shot a home movie with his Victor 16.

After an hour they packed up and headed for Gun Lake, where Ed stopped and bought a crate of bootleg whiskey from three, as he put it, "Italian gentlemen from Chicago." With the contraband booze safely hidden in the trunk, Ed and Verna made it to Schuler's Hotel and Restaurant in Marshall by 5 p.m. The Bentz registered as "Mr. & Mrs. Edw. Dewey, Detroit" and retired to their second floor room for a nap and bath before dinner.

Ed and Verna dressed for dinner, she in a silver lame backless gown that showed her slim figure to its best advantage and he in a broad-shouldered Palm Beach blazer and slacks. Heads turned as they descended the golden oak staircase and Ed whispered to Verna that she looked like a million bucks. The radio was on in the parlor and Kate Smith was singing Verna's favorite song, *Dream a Little Dream of Me*. Mrs. Bentzs gave her husband's arm a squeeze as they were shown to their table.

A meal at Schuler's was always a feast. Ed and Verna started by sharing a large appetizer tray filled with cheddar cheese, creamed herring, corn relish, cinnamon apple rings, chicken liver pate, and venison meatballs in a spicy sauce, accompanied by a little basket of cheese Bisquicks straight from the oven. For his entree Ed ordered the house specialty prime rib and Verna choose fresh walleye.

They were waiting for their orange sherbert desserts when the proprietor, Albert Schuler, stopped at their table to ask if they were enjoying their meal. He apologized for not checking with them earlier, but he had been called out to deal with a local police matter. Schuler explained that he was a deputy sheriff as well as a restaurateur, and "Summertime can get a little hairy when the 'gangsters' arrive from Chicago and South Bend."

"Oh, how absolutely exciting your life must be!" Verna fawned as she reached out and touched the proprietor's elbow. She turned to Ed and exclaimed, "Don't you agree, Honey?"

Ed furrowed his brow and, looking Schuler straight in the eye, solemnly announced, "It's a good thing for folks like us that the police stay on top of things in these perilous times."

Schuler grinned from ear to ear, shook Ed's hand and announced to the "nice couple" that their dessert would be "on the house." With a small bow, he left for the next table. Verna pretended to wipe her mouth with her napkin to hide a giggle. Ed just shook his head.

After dessert, they took a stroll down Michigan Avenue so that Ed could have a cigar. They stopped at a small park and sat for a spell to watch the spray dance from a fountain that had been built to resemble a small Doric temple. The night sky was clear and Verna started to count, out loud, the shooting stars. After a minute, Ed reached into his pocket and produced a small velvet-covered box, which he handed to his wife.

"I never gave you a diamond, sweetheart, and for that I'm truly sorry. I was hoping you might wear this as a keepsake of our summers on Lake Michigan."

Verna slowly opened the little box and there, gleaming in the moonlight, was Ed's new Double Eagle affixed to a length of gold chain. He gently fastened the necklace around her dainty neck.

She gave her big husband a small kiss and said, "This will bring us good luck on our move to Nevada. I'm sure of it." He gave her his arm and they walked back to the hotel while she hummed *Dream a Little Dream.*

Upon retiring Ed read aloud from a new copy of *God's Little Acre* while Verna snuggled next to him and pretended to be scandalized. Later, in the dark, she turned toward him and said, "Eddie, I need you to promise me something."

Bentz, half asleep, mumbled, "Anything, lover, anything."

She punched him awake and said, quite seriously, "Really listen to what I have to say for a change; this is important!"

Having been married long enough to know something

was up, he rubbed his face and said, "You have my complete attention."

"Well, you know I've grown very fond of Helen and Ronnie and Darlene." He said nothing so she continued. "Helen is deathly scared that Lester is not up to pulling off whatever it is the two of you have cooking. I need you to promise me that you will not let him ruin their life with some horrible mistake."

Bentz took a deep breath, exhaled toward the ceiling, and in his most convincing tone replied, "Sweetheart, I promise I won't let Lester shoot himself, or anybody else, in the foot. Trust me, you know I've delivered this baby a hundred times before." His reward was a deep kiss, which brought him to full readiness.

They awoke to the bells of St. Mary's Church calling parishioners to Mass across the street. After a breakfast of warm pastry and hot coffee the Bentzs loaded Ed's Packard and drove east. The trip home began with a southeasterly leg through Hillsdale, then south on Highway 127 into Ohio, followed by a backtrack west through northern Indiana. They bought a pie for lunch from an Amish woman outside Goshen, and then Ed sped

on past LaPorte and back to Long Beach while Verna napped.

Before Ed had fully unpacked the car, Verna was headed down

the beach to reassure her friend.

Chapter Eleven

August 12 to 15, 1933

The dog days of summer became unbearably hot. The radio reported that a world record high temperature had been recorded in Mexico, and the entire United States was suffering a wave of heat and humidity. In Long Beach the breeze off Lake Michigan provided some relief, but on still afternoons Ed Bentz caught himself wishing it were September.

The car for the Grand Haven job rolled up to the Gillis cottage on a Saturday morning. It was a 1930 Buick sedan Series 40, with suicide doors and a distinctive exterior sun shade across the top of the windshield. The dark blue finish was faded, the side-mount spare tires were missing, and one of the headlamps was cracked. The running board on the passenger's side was riddled with several suspicious holes. Gillis walked the driver over to the Bentz cottage, noticed that Ed was standing on the beach smoking a cigar, and strolled over to make introductions.

"Big Ed, this here is Freddie Monahan. He and I did a little business when he drove for the Touhy brothers."

Freddie was a few years older than Gillis, extremely thin, and had a long face with almost no chin. He was missing the two middle fingers of his right hand, which he tended to keep lowered at his side. Freddie had a hard time meeting another man's gaze and usually stared at the ground when speaking. When Bentz shook Freddie's left hand he was put off by the thin man's limp grip. Ed immediately disliked Freddie so he squeezed harder than need be before releasing the good hand to its squirming owner.

"Freddie gave me a real good deal on the car, and he's willing to drive as our fifth man." Lester blurted out the last bit, and waited for Ed's approval.

Ed took a few steps uphill until he could see Freddie's car. He was not impressed.

"Can you shoot?" demanded Bentz.

"Not so good 'cus I'm right handed," admitted the anxious Freddie. "But I hold my own with a knife!"

"Know how to sweep a street?" Bentz was referring to a lookout's job.

Freddie appeared perplexed by the question and said nothing.

Bentz turned his back on Freddie, leaned over Gillis and said, "Hell's bells, Lester, you don't take on a greenhorn as your wheel man just to save a few dollars on a used car! How do you know this character will come through in a pinch? Is he smart enough to learn the get?"

Instead of becoming angry, Gillis tried to reassure Bentz. "Freddie will never let me down because he's afraid of what I'll do to him if he does. He's not much of a fighter but at least he's smart enough to memorize directions. C'mon Ed, I've trusted you, and now you gotta trust me."

Bentz looked out at the darkening waves and pondered the little man's argument. "What the hell," he concluded, "it's Lester's neck, not mine."

Bentz turned to Freddie, who took an involuntary step backward from the big man. "You can stay with Lester and Helen. Tomorrow you learn the way home. And get that damn headlamp fixed!" Bentz turned on a heel and strode back to his cottage in silence.

Starting the Saturday Freddie arrived in Long Beach there was a thunderstorm every afternoon or evening for three straight days. It would only rain an hour or two at a time, but between storms the big lake remained choppy and dark. The unseasonably high temperatures were tempered by the rain, but the increased humidity was almost worse than the dry heat.

Lester made short work of introducing Freddie to the rest of the troupe and to Teddy, who was back in Long Beach to escape the scorching streets of Chicago. To Ed's secret annoyance, Teddy seemed to think Freddie was a barrel of laughs, perhaps because it was so easy to make nervous Freddie the butt of every joke. Freddie turned out to be an apt pupil at learning the get, and after Bentz was satisfied that Monahan could find his way to and from Grand Haven without deviation from the plan, Ed decided to stop worrying about the skinny creep.

Professor Bentz' last lecture was about the mechanics of the actual robbery. A street map of Grand Haven and Ed's own drawing of the inside of the bank were spread across the kitchen table in the Gillis cottage. The five would-be bank robbers and Teddy were perched on chairs around the maps while Ed remained standing. Bentz used his putter as a pointer.

"Time is your enemy. The city police station and the county sheriff's office are just up the street from the bank. Assume an alarm will go off. You need to get in, load up, and be back in the car in under five minutes. If you lollygaggle, chances are you will never make it back to Long Beach." Ed had the complete attention of the room.

"Lester and Earl will be dropped off at Fourth and Franklin. They will walk north to Washington and then west to the front door of the bank. Tommy and Chuck will get out at Third and Franklin, walk up the west side of the bank, turn and come in the front door right behind Lester and Earl." He pointed the putter at Gillis and said "*If* you had a sixth man, he would be with Caroll and Fisher and stop at the back door of the bank next to the alley." Gillis said nothing so Bentz continued.

"Freddie will follow Franklin to Second, turn north and cross Washington, turn east at Columbus, and then come back south on Third. He will park at the curb next to the post office and wait for Lester's signal." Bentz gave Freddie his coldest stare and said "Do. . . *not*. . . move. . . until you see Lester!"

Freddie swallowed hard and croaked "OK."

Gillis started to fidget and asked, "What guns?"

"All four who go inside will wear a pistol. Leave one of the Thompsons in the car and put the other in a picnic basket with one of the riot guns. Once you get inside, Lester will take the

Thompson and Earl will carry the twelve gauge. The Winchesters can stay in the car because they are no good for close up work.

"Tommy will guard the front door and Earl the back. Chuck will skim the teller's cages of all cash, coin, bonds and traveler's checks. Just dump everything in a bag as fast as you can. If need be, Lester will persuade the cashier to open the vault. There should be more cash inside the vault, but don't forget to also take every bond and important looking paper. My little brother has a knack for turning those things into cash.

"Don't call each other by name, and yell when you speak to the employees. Do not make them put their hands up. Instead have the tellers and such kneel or lie on the floor. Close the curtains if you have time. Tomorrow Helen is going to pick up some light cotton gloves; make sure to wear them so you don't leave prints."

"Alvin told me," to everyone's surprise the speaker was Caroll, "that on the way out we should grab one of the lady tellers an' make her stand on the runnin' board until we are several blocks gone, then slow down and push her off. Alvin said the cops won't take a shot at you while a woman is hanging on for dear life and screaming her fool head off." There was a murmur of agreement from the others.

Bentz frowned and exhaled slowly. "Alvin has become reckless because he spends too much time with the Barker brothers. No, you leave the women alone! If you need a hostage or two on the road, it's men only." Tommy shrugged but said nothing. The room was quiet.

"Any questions?" Bentz asked.

"Just one," said Gillis with a straight face. "Ain't you gonna' be sorry you missed the party?" That prompted a round of hoots and hollers.

"I'll live."

With that said, Bentz had the class follow him down to the beach where he drew a full scale floor plan in the sand and made the bandits practice their moves. They caught on quickly.

Teddy watched his brother barking orders and thought,

"If Rockne's job is still open, Big Brother, you should apply."

Chapter Twelve

August 17, 1933

Lester sent Helen into town to buy groceries and two of the largest picnic baskets she could find. When Helen returned, Verna wandered over to the Gillis cottage for a chat and ended up helping Helen pack a large lunch for Lester to take with him the following morning. They then took the kids for a short march up and down the beach to pick up such treasures as driftwood, small stones and the occasional feather. By mid afternoon an ominous swath of dark grey appeared where the waves met the sky, so Verna invited Helen to come back to the Bentz cottage for coffee and cookies.

"If the end of the world began on a Thursday afternoon, it would look like that," remarked Verna as she pointed at the horizon with her coffee cup.

Ed, who had been unsuccessfully trying to read with the Gillis children playing around his feet, stood and announced, "In that case, this must be my chance for one last swim." He changed in the bedroom and headed for the beach with a towel around his neck. After a moment Helen excused herself, gathered up the kids and was out the door.

Ed could see Teddy coming out of the Gillis cottage and waved his brother to join him. Teddy obediently ran across the dune to stand with him.

"So, is Lester all packed and ready for tomorrow?" Ed inquired as he surveyed the darkening sky.

"Seems like it," answered Teddy.

"When he gets back, you and I will need to inventory the take and put you on the road right away to peddle the product. You want to start selling before the police have a chance to blow the whistle." Ed was more or less talking to himself, as the drill was well known to both brothers.

"About that, Ed; well, Lester says that if I tag along as the sixth man he'll cut me in for a full share. I could really use the money," he whined.

Ed stiffened, then turned to pull within a few inches of Teddy. "You dumb ass, that little shit could get you killed! What if he flies off the handle and shoots somebody? The cops will never stop looking for you."

For the first time in his life Teddy tried to stand up to his big brother. "Easy for you to say, always the big man, always in for the big score! Well, it's my turn to make hay now. For three months I've been kissing your ass and Lester's ass to make this deal happen. I'm tired of it; I want to be treated fairly and not like some errand boy!" Teddy was almost shouting by the end of his speech, with fists clenched.

Instead of yelling back, Ed wrapped an arm around Teddy's shoulders and said in a low voice, "You are my brother. Blood sticks with blood, remember?" Ed released Teddy and faced him. "The big money will be in the bonds, and a small time crook like Gillis will only want the cash. I need you to stay away from the bank so nobody has your description when you pass paper. Promise me you'll drive back to Chicago first thing in the morning."

Teddy said nothing for a moment, then looked down at the sand and muttered, "It's kinda your fault anyway; Lester said you've been nuts about a sixth man so the troupe needs me. It felt good to be needed."

"I will smooth things with Lester," Ed promised.

"OK," Teddy replied with a weak smile. Looking almost relieved, he turned and headed back up the hill with his back to the rising wind.

For a moment, Bentz thought about queering the whole deal. "Better turn this over for a few minutes," he told himself.

With his thoughts flying, Bentz strode into the building waves and began a crawl stroke past the first sandbar and out to the second. When he tried to stand, he was unable to find good footing and instead slipped beneath the surface. He could feel a rushing undertow pulling him beyond the bar and out to deep water. Bentz had swum into hidden currents before, but never one with such a malevolent grip. Ed felt a twinge of panic in his throat as his lungs started to burn for lack of air and the deepening water turned dark purple. He closed his eyes and a memory of Verna filled his consciousness.

It was a year ago, May, perhaps early June. She was reclining on the beach with her head back and her legs drawn up slightly at the knees, and she was laughingly calling out, "Ed, Ed, come sit next to me." A calmness came over Bentz and he willed himself to stop fighting the current so his torso would bob to the top of the whitecaps. When his upturned face broke the surface Ed sucked in three huge gulps of moist air, and with renewed strength began swimming parallel to the shore until he once again felt in control.

Propelled by several large kicks the big man turned toward shore and found the first sandbar. He dug his toes into the sandy bottom and stood with the waves crashing at his back, hands on his hips, while he coughed and spit until his head cleared. He could see porch lights coming on at the cottages. A minute passed, maybe two, and then he was ready to make his break. Taking a deep breath, Ed dove into a passing wave and after a few powerful strokes was pushed safely back to the beach.

Ed did not bother to towel off but marched right up to the front door of the Gillis cottage. He could see Lester and Helen through the screen. They were packing a large picnic hamper. Breathing heavily, and not bothering to knock, Bentz swung open the screen door and stepped inside. He stared at Lester, water pooling on the linoleum around Ed's sandy feet.

"Ed, can we help . . ." Helen started.

"Teddy stays home. I go. Tomorrow I call the shots." Bentz did not wait for an objection but turned and banged the screen open as he left.

Lester and Helen glanced at each other, then turned to watch Bentz march up the beach. When the big redhead was out of sight Helen looked back at Lester, laughed and said, "I told you the old boy wouldn't let his idiot brother tag along!"

Gillis grabbed his wife around the waist and exclaimed,

"You, little girl, are still the brains of this outfit!"

Chapter Thirteen

August 18, 1933

A day off was rare for Grand Haven Police Chief
Lawrence DeWitt, so the Chief made sure to make the most of
this one. The DeWitt family had arisen early to drive the sixty-
five miles from Grand Haven to Ionia and take in the Free Fair.
By midafternoon they had strolled through the merchant
exhibitions, watched a horse pull, and examined most of the 4-H
displays. After a rest in the shade they would tour what was
billed as the Midwest's Greatest Midway. The usually somber
chief loosened his collar and gave his oldest daughter some

change to buy cotton candy for the entire family. They would be home in time for a restful night's sleep.

Chief DeWitt was five feet, eight inches tall, barrel chested, with thinning grey hair that he combed over from left to right. He had a prominent nose and piercing grey eyes. His standard daily garb was a grey tweed suit with vest, adorned only by a small pocket watch and chain. He never appeared in uniform except for special occasions. On this trip to the fair he had shed his coat and vest.

The forty-three-year-old DeWitt was usually on duty fourteen hours a day, seven days a week, and his four officers worked ten-hour shifts, seven days a week. DeWitt's office was on the second floor of City Hall, next to the offices of the manager and clerk. City Hall was a two-story brick building that had housed a horse-drawn steam pumper and a horse-drawn hook-n-ladder wagon in its first floor garage for almost five decades. The ladder wagon and two horses still occupied one of the stalls, but the other was now home to a 1925 American LaFrance fire truck. The department's 1925 Maxwell police car was parked outside when not on patrol. Perched as it was on the southwest corner of Washington and Fifth, City Hall was just a stone's throw from the courthouse and the county sheriff's office.

That afternoon, patrolman Ferdi Kinkema had driven the Maxwell out to the beach to investigate a suspicious-person complaint, so patrolman Clarence Van Toll was minding the office and catching up on his filing. The Chief was a stickler for paperwork so Van Toll used slow days to put his reports in good order.

Ottawa County Sheriff Ben Rosema was also gone from his Grand Haven residence-office that Friday afternoon, but on official business. The sheriff was planning to lead a raid on a nudist colony that had sprung up that summer on a farm near Zeeland, and the sheriff intended to brief the heads of the local police departments that would assist.

Rosema's twenty-two-year-old son Maury was a deputy sheriff, and when his father left for Zeeland Maury quipped, "Dad, make sure you cover all the important parts."

Undersheriff Ed Rycenga, who was sitting at the next desk, choked back a laugh and almost spilled his coffee.

The big Buick rumbled through Holland slightly before noon without stopping, and now was zipping along the road north to Grand Haven. At that juncture Highway 31 ran parallel to the Grand Trunk railway line. The rail bed seemed to rise as the car approached the Pigeon River, but in fact the road was slipping down into a cedar swamp that had been created by a thousand years of meandering water. At the bridge the road was flanked by two immense white pines, survivors of the towering conifer forest that had disappeared when the county was logged to rebuild Chicago after the famous fire.

Rolling across the bridge and climbing upward for a few seconds, the sedan came to an intersection and stopped. The milepost next to the tracks read *West Olive*. A tiny general store and filling station stood sentry at the corner. The Buick slowly pulled through the intersection and came to rest again in front of the pump. The driver's door opened and a big redheaded man emerged and stretched. A pimply-faced kid in dungarees was lounging on a bench in front of the filling station. The driver told him, "Fill 'er up, and check the tires," and then ambled into the store.

The proprietor was in hot pursuit of an extremely large horsefly. He had a ragged flyswatter in one hand and a bottle of Vernors in the other. "Be right with you, friend," he said without taking his eyes off his quarry.

Finally, with a slap and a "gotcha," the hunt was over.

As the storekeeper opened the screen door to discard his prize, Ed Bentz smiled and asked, "What's the limit on those things?"

The merchant looked at Bentz, decided immediately that he liked the big stranger, and replied, "As many as you can eat in one sitting." They shared a laugh.

"Need anything besides gas, friend?" asked the merchant.

"No, that'll do," Bentz answered. "But I and my associates have been on the road since sun-up and need to stretch our legs before we head to Saginaw. Does that little river end up in Lake Michigan? Thought I'd stick my big toe in the water before going on."

"Oh sure, just turn around and go to your right at the stop sign. After a mile or two you'll dead end near the ruins of the old Ottawa House Hotel. At that point you can take an easy walk along the bank of Pigeon Lake or hike to the big lake if you're ambitious."

The kid stumbled in to report the sale and announce that the tires looked good to him. Bentz paid for the gas, flipped the kid two bits for "doing such a fine job on the windshield", and slid behind the wheel.

As the Buick came about and then turned west the kid remarked to his boss, "Them fellers must be goin' to an undertakers' convention because they looked pretty severe."

"Well," replied the proprietor, "a long car trip on a hot day tends to put a person in a foul mood. Still, that big fella seemed to be enjoyin' himself."

Three weeks previously Bentz had inspected the side roads of West Olive and he had a destination in mind. The road surface changed from macadam to gravel as the troupe from Long Beach motored by a CCC crew of perhaps fifty men. They were planting rows of red pine saplings in the sandy soil of the small hills that separated the road from the river.

"That looks like hot work," mused Chuck Fisher from the back seat.

"That's the choice today, boys," replied Lester from the front, "break your back or break a bank."

Everyone laughed at the joke but Freddie. Straddling the hump between Ed and Lester on the front seat, Freddie had remained silent since Benton Harbor. Bentz suspected that Lester's choice for wheel man was a little carsick.

Another mile of gravel had passed under the wheels when Bentz turned off the road and pulled in beside a little farmhouse with a Dutch gambrel roof. There was a foreclosure notice posted on the front porch. Leaving the motor running, Ed got out and walked to the door. He peered inside to make sure the place was empty. Satisfied, he got back in the car and drove past a small barn and then to the woods beyond. The Buick came to a stop in a circle of sassafras saplings and the crew of bandits clambered out.

"Time to drain the water off the lily," announced Lester, and he disappeared behind an oak. The others more or less followed suit. Fisher opened the trunk and removed a large picnic basket stuffed with sandwiches and Mason jars filled with lemonade. Each of the men devoured at least two sandwiches, except for Freddie. He declined all food and just sipped on some lukewarm coffee.

"Let's suit up," Bentz ordered. All but Freddie stripped off their shirts and helped each other tie on the bullet proof vests. When they redressed, Ed took off his golf shirt, slacks and loafers and replaced them with clean denim overalls, an old undershirt, and a pair of clodhoppers.

"Good gosh, Ed, you look like you belong with them CCC fellas plantin' trees," quipped Gillis.

"That's the point, boys, just trying to blend in."

Caroll and Fisher looked at each other's new grey-blue suits, bought for the occasion in Michigan City, and silently wondered if they had made a tactical error. Caroll's white straw boater and Fisher's black fedora were the only noticeable difference between their ensembles. Gillis, dressed in an open-collar mint green shirt, grey slacks and his old newsboy cap, could care less about Big Ed's costuming theories. Doyle, who had taken forever to strap on a vest under his black suit coat, was still fumbling with his tie.

Next they turned their attention to the weapons. One of the Thompsons, minus its stock, was loaded with a fifty-round drum and placed in the bottom of the picnic basket. Lester put a twenty-round square in a front pocket. Caroll loaded the riot gun with rounds of buckshot and put it in the basket next to the Tommy gun. Gillis, Doyle, Caroll and Fisher each concealed a thirty-eight Super pistol inside their clothes. Bentz slid his thirty-eight snub-nose into a side pocket of his overalls. One of the rifles was loaded and placed on the floor under the front seat. Three cotton laundry bags were removed from the trunk, two stuffed inside the third, and then thrown on the back seat. A second Tommy gun, several more rifles, and hundreds of rounds of ammunition remained in the trunk alongside two cans of gasoline and a box of roofing nails.

After a final trip to the woods the men climbed back aboard the Buick, with Freddie behind the wheel. They returned to the main highway and headed north to work.

It had been a busy day for Yetta Bonema. Since mid-morning she had babysat the Miller boys while her best friend, Emma Miller, visited another young wife at the maternity room of Hatton Hospital. Since lunch, Yetta's daughter Barbara had been toddling after the older Miller children as fast as her little legs would take her. The oldest Miller boy put his two younger brothers through their paces with tag and other chase games, which involved a lot of door slamming and gleeful shrieking by Barbara. Next the boys tried unsuccessfully to round up the litter of half-grown kittens that lived out in the tool shed. When the joy of teasing cats wore off, the boys took turns pushing a scooter around the garden while Barbara gave chase carrying her favorite toy – a metal casting of Mickey and Minnie Mouse aboard a bright red motorcycle. For a two year old with a vocabulary of perhaps three dozen words, Barbara could evoke a very impressive engine noise.

Eventually Yetta bribed Barbara and the two younger boys to go down for a nap with a promise of a trip to the beach. Barbara's older brother had walked to the beach that morning to spend the day with friends, and Yetta had promised to pick him up at 4 p.m. Nap time gave Yetta the opportunity to pack a big canvas bag with a purse, towels, a thermos of water, gardening tools for digging in the sand, and, of course, the Mickey Mouse motorcycle.

The kids woke up and at Yetta's urging tromped one by one to the toilet. Yetta pulled a swim dress over the squirming Barbara (the boys would swim in their short pants). She loaded the kids into the back seat of her husband's black Chevrolet Confederate, tossed her beach bag on the front seat, and put the big sedan in gear.

"Momma, Mickey!" demanded Barbara. Yetta passed the shiny toy over the seat to her daughter and set off to pick up Emma.

Chapter Fourteen

August 18, 1933

Leoria VanDyke habitually began sweeping the floors of the bank a half hour before closing time. At 2:30 in the afternoon, there was abundant natural light streaming through the tall exterior windows, which made it easier to spot the grains of sand that had been tracked in by the customers. When Leoria finished you could eat off the floor. It was a tidy way to end the week.

The six full-time employees of the bank were starting to go through their daily routine of closing up shop. Assistant cashier Will Pellegrom, savings teller Martha Meschke, and commercial teller Art Welling were balancing their cash drawers before handing them over to cashier F.C. 'Ted' Bolt for a second count and night storage in the vault. The bookkeeper, Vera Correll, was tying up her ledgers; she would give them to Bolt for overnight safekeeping as well.

Martha was being slowed down by Pete VanLopik, a customer who made a point of stopping by every Friday to make a business deposit at Welling's station. While Welling counted out the deposit VanLopik always tried to chat up Miss Meschke. VanLopik was wasting his time, because Martha only had eyes for Will.

Will was likewise smitten with Martha. A week ago Will had finally summoned the courage to ask Martha out, and much to his delight she said yes. After work they were going to enjoy a chicken dinner at the Ferry Hotel, and then stroll next door to the Grand Theater to watch Edward G. Robinson and Mary Astor in *The Little Giant*. Will had brought his old valise to work, stuffed with a fresh shirt for him and a small box of cordials for Martha. The bag was stashed on the floor between his station and Martha's station.

Auditor Jonnie Lindemulder was in Ted Bolt's corner office helping the cashier inventory a stack of *Chicago, St. Paul & Milwaukee* railroad bonds. Those securities were to be transported by Brinks armored car to The Northern Trust in Chicago on Monday morning, and the count had to be verified by two bank employees. Lindemulder's attention wandered, and his boss was not happy when they had to start the count over. Bolt wanted to close up on time because the Masonic Lodge was throwing a party that was to begin promptly at 7 p.m. Ted was looking forward to a little excitement in what had otherwise been a hot, humid and slow week. "Pay attention, Jonnie," growled Bolt, "so that we can both get home before midnight!"

Martha looked like she could use rescuing from a gabby customer, so Will strolled over to her window under the pretense of asking for some singles. The disappointed customer headed for the front door but had to step aside for four men who suddenly marched inside, one after the other, just a few minutes before the town clock across the street would strike three.

Pellegrom noticed that one of the men was carrying a woven basket with what appeared to be fishing tackle stuffed inside. "Probably a tourist who needs cash to buy bait," thought Pellegrom as he returned to the cashier's window.

The last man through the door, sporting dark hair and darker eyes, scowled at Peter VanLopik and would not let him pass.

Art Welling, wearing a bright yellow vest trimmed with blue buttons, started humming the refrain of *The Victors.* Tall and athletic, Welling had played football for the Michigan Wolverines a few years back and was overjoyed when his alma mater won the national championship in 1932. Still, Martha wished Art would learn a new favorite.

Martha's irritation with Art distracted her from noticing the men who had come in through the front door. She only looked up from her counting when she heard a deep voice right in front of her teller window say, "Leave all the money on the counter, missy, and this is no joke! Stay right where you are and don't move. If you move I will shoot. If you try to push an alarm I will shoot."

Pointed directly at her midsection was the largest, blackest pistol she could imagine. The robber pointing the gun at her was at least six feet tall, muscular, sported a broken nose, and wore a white straw hat. He motioned with the gun and Martha hurried out from behind her teller's cage to stand with Vera. A second robber, short and with the clean-shaven face of an adolescent, was pointing a pistol at Will. Martha's eyes darted about and she nearly panicked when she realized a third thug, looking like a tree stump in a black double breasted suit, was blocking the front door. He was keeping Bolt and Lindemulder covered with a pistol.

As soon as Martha left her teller station Will started feeling with his toe for the silent alarm that was built into the floor between his station and hers. Try as he might, Will could not find the safety cap that he needed to kick aside before depressing the button. With horror, Pellegrom realized that he had set his valise directly over the safety cap. Will clenched the counter for leverage and tried to hook the bag's handle with his toe, but before he could make the connection he was grabbed by the shoulder and dragged out of his station.

Pellegrom's assailant was a big man dressed in overalls and wearing no hat to cover his curly red hair. The redhead held the terrified Pellegrom in one hand and a large basket in the other. He easily pushed Pellegrom to the floor, then turned and strode to the back door. He unlocked the deadbolt so that a fifth man, wearing a black fedora, could enter with a blue laundry bag slung over his shoulder.

Returning to the middle of the room, the redheaded crook reached into his basket and pulled out a shotgun, which he handed to the stocky man in the black suit. He then slid the basket across the floor to the short robber. The little man reached into the basket and pulled out a Tommy gun, which he proceeded to wave at all of the terrified bank employees but no one in particular.

"Do not," warned Mr. Overalls, "upset my little friend. Everybody on the floor!"

The robbers wearing the fedora and the straw hat quickly herded the rest of the bank employees and VanLopik into the middle of the main room. All of the captives but Ted Bolt were made to lie face down on the stone floor. The robber in the fedora pulled a second laundry bag from the first and tossed it to the bandit in the straw hat. While the short bandit kept everyone covered with the Tommy gun and the stocky crook stood guard at the front door with his shotgun, the man in the straw hat and his confederate in the fedora methodically cleaned out the four teller cages, closing window curtains as they went. All of the loot was dumped unceremoniously into the laundry bags. The redhead spotted the railroad bonds on Bolt's desk and yelled at the man in the straw hat to "Clean that corner desk!" The bonds were immediately stuffed into a bag with the counter loot.

"Now," the redhead smiled at Bolt, "let's see the vault!"

Leoria VanDyke was hanging her broom in the janitor's closet when she first heard the shouting and cursing out on the main floor of the bank. For a split second she froze, but then had the presence of mind to slip inside the small closet. There was not enough room to close the door tight, so she held on to the knob and watched what happened next through a very slim crack.

Mr. Bolt came into view. He had his hands at his sides and was being followed by a big redheaded man wearing overalls and holding a small black revolver. Bringing up the rear was a rough-looking fellow in a straw hat, carrying a laundry bag in one hand and a pistol in the other. The three paraded by the closet and stopped at the closed door of the vault.

"Open it," barked the man in the overalls. He stuck his revolver in Bolt's back for emphasis. The cashier slowly dropped to one knee and gave the top dial three quick spins to the left. He then moved to the bottom dial and slowly started to work a back and forth combination. He paused several times to wipe his hand on his shirt. The big robber suddenly cursed and shoved Bolt side. He looked at his partner and said, "Fetch the young guy in the yellow vest!"

The other robber did as he was ordered and soon returned pushing Welling before him with his pistol. The robber in the overalls looked Welling square in the eye and growled, "Unlock this damn door right now, or I will shoot your boss through his bald head!"

Welling leaped to the task and had the door wide open in under ten seconds. The redheaded outlaw grabbed Bolt by the collar and dragged him inside the vault, where the cashier was forced to fill a laundry bag with cash and a few books of travelers checks. As the two men exited the vault an unfamiliar voice out in the lobby yelled, "Big Ed, we got a rank!"

❧

Chapter Fifteen

August 18, 1933

The three-story brick Masonic Temple Building was directly across Third Street from the bank. McLellen's five-and-dime was on the first floor, where twenty-one-year-old Chuck Bugielski was the assistant manager.

Bugielski was making change for a fresh-faced Coast Guard lieutenant (junior grade) who had strolled in to buy some penny postcards. "So how do you like your new boat?" he asked the off-duty officer.

"Oh, she's a peach, she is!" replied the young man.

"Built for speed, not just ice breaking, by those boys in Bay City." The shiny white cutter *Escanaba* had been stationed in Grand Haven for not quite a year, and its crew and their families had been welcomed with open arms by the community. The young officer accepted his change and slipped it inside his khaki uniform blouse.

"Well, I hear you boys had some rough times during your first winter," Bugielski continued.

"That's true," replied the customer, "but as they say, you hafta go out but ya don't hafta come back!" He turned with a grin and strolled out the front door to Washington Street.

"Lucky stiff," thought Bugielski. "I bet the girls really go for that uniform!"

As the Coastie left through the front door, three boys of grammar school age piled in through the side door. "Hi, Mr. B, can we have five cents of Red Hots?" asked the boy in the lead.

"Sure thing, Gene," replied Bugielski. "And what are you rascals up to this afternoon?" Bugielski had parked his Chevrolet convertible behind the store as usual, but had not bothered to put the top up. He did not want the boys to play at being Barney Oldfield in his clean car.

"We're playin' cops and robbers," exclaimed Gene Rothi, aged twelve years and obviously the leader of the gang, "an' Red Hots are gonna be the loot!" A grubby nickel was solemnly exchanged for the paper bag of spicy candy, and the boys were out the side door again with a whoop. As the glass door swung shut Chuck could see across the street to the rear door of People's Bank. A burly man with a blue laundry bag over his shoulder was being let in. That made Bugielski take notice of the time.

"Hey, Alice," Bugielski called to his counter girl, "watch the till while I make the night deposit at the bank." Chuck reached under the brass-plated National for the night deposit pouch, gave a thumbs-up to Alice, and exited through the side door. As was his routine, Bugielski would stroll over to the bank at 3 p.m. and tap on the back door. Art Welling would unlock the door and accept the store's daily deposit, and if Art's boss were not in sight the two young bachelors would take a moment to discuss their plans for the weekend.

The heat outside was brutal. The merchant could feel the sweat start to trickle down his neck even before he started across the street. As Bugielski stepped off the curb he waved to 'Captain' Pleines, a retired Army officer who had served in China during the Boxer Rebellion, in the Philippines, and as a training officer during the Great War. Never one to be idle, Pleines was washing windows at the Elks Club.

As the clock in the tower of the First Reformed Church began to chime three o'clock a large black Buick came flying out of nowhere, roared past the startled Bugielski, and then turned onto Franklin and disappeared going east. After trading shakes of the head with Pleines, Bugielski reached the back door of the bank and knocked. Nobody answered. He knocked again. Still no answer. He tried the handle and the door wouldn't budge. Bugielski stepped back a pace so he could peer down the sidewalk and across Washington Street to the clock tower. 3:03 was the time. The click of the deadbolt brought his attention back to the door, and that's when he heard the bushes whisper, "For God's sake, Chuck, get down – it's a bank robbery!"

Ed 'Cotty' Kinkema was so named for his head of white hair, but otherwise he strongly resembled his cousin, Ted Bolt. Both men were solidly built, with large eyes, broad noses, and strong chins. "Cotty" was a bit beefier, which came in handy when he loaded and delivered furniture from Addison's furniture store.

Addison's was right next door to People's Bank, and when Cotty became the store manager his cousin Ted convinced Cotty to place an alarm bell in Cotty's office. Kinkema never shied away from a scrap, and Bolt knew his cousin would come in handy in an emergency. If the bank's alarm was triggered, bells would also go off at the city police station and at the county sheriff's office, both of which were up the street from the bank. But Bolt could count on his cousin to arrive first and well-armed. Kinkema kept a Browning Auto-5 in his office closet, loaded with buckshot.

Kinkema had just returned from delivering a load of bedding to the Nat Robbins house at the top of the hill. The mattresses had to be wrestled up three flights of stairs in the servants' stairwell and Kinkema was still lathered up from the effort. He sat down at his desk with a Coca-Cola in his meaty right hand, leaned back and closed his eyes with a contented "Ah". The Coke bottle was not very cold, so he made a mental note to put more ice in the cooler.

A second later the soda bottle flew out of his grasp as Kinkema was startled to his feet by the bank's alarm bell. "Hell in a hand basket!" he mumbled while reaching for the shotgun. He could not find the box of extra shells. Cursing softly, he swung around and rumbled though the kitchenette display, past the sofas, and slammed through the front door armed with five rounds and a bad attitude.

Bursting into the afternoon sun, Kinkema immediately noticed a big Buick sedan stopped at the curb next to the post office with its motor running. The driver made eye contact with Kinkema and the blood drained from his face when he saw Cotty's shotgun. The Buick lurched into motion, ran through the intersection against a red light, turned east at Franklin, sped past the Robbins house and out of town.

Kinkema spun on his heel and ran back through the store and onto the loading dock. Crouched over and breathing heavily, he eased his head and shoulders out into the alley that ran behind the furniture store and the bank. Kinkema turned to the right and made a beeline for the rear corner of the bank. He almost stumbled over three boys who were sitting in the shade of the alley, their eyes wide and their mouths stuffed full of candy. The kids scattered as Kinkema dropped to a knee behind some bushes. Slowly poking his head up so that he could see around the corner of the building, Kinkema was surprised to see Chuck Bugielski rattling the back door of the bank. Cotty was almost close enough to poke Chuck with the end of his shotgun. Then he heard the door's deadbolt click open from the inside.

Kinkema gave a hoarse whisper for Bugielski to take cover, and then retreated across Third to the side exit of McLellan's. Bugielski quickly followed. The two men crouched in the recessed doorway, breathing heavily.

"I have a pistol in my car," Chuck whispered.

"Get it quick," urged Cotty.

Bugielski ran stooped over to the trunk of his car and slowly raised the lid. He felt with his left hand for a small toolbox and was just able to reach it with his outstretched fingers. He opened the box by touch and removed the loaded revolver that was stored inside. By this time he had been joined by Captain Pleines.

"What the hell . . . " Pleines began, but was stopped short by the sight of about a dozen people filing out the back door of the bank.

Ted Bolt's three rapid spins of the top dial on the vault door had set off an alarm at the police station and at the sheriff's residence. Ed Rycenga was on the phone with a bailiff at the courthouse and Maury Rosema had just returned from making rounds inside the cellblock of the jail. Rycenga dropped the receiver and ran to the gun locker, where he was soon joined by Rosema. They each removed a Winchester Model 97 pump shotgun from the rack, and Rosema grabbed a canvas shoulder bag of extra shells filled with buckshot. They sprinted to one of the department's 1930 Nash Single Six patrol cars, jumped into the front seat, turned on the siren and raced at top speed for the corner of Washington and Third.

When the alarm went off in the police office at City Hall, Clarence Van Toll thought it must be some sort of malfunction. He changed his mind when he heard the siren start up on the sheriff department's Nash. It took Van Toll a few frantic moments of rummaging through the Chief's desk to find the spare key to the gun rack. He finally found the key, took a shotgun off the wall, ran down the stairs and turned toward the bank with his Winchester at port arms. By the time he reached Fourth Street he could hear gunshots.

*

Chapter Sixteen

August 18, 1933

When Gillis shouted his warning to Bentz he was standing at a window with the curtain drawn. Inquisitive civilians had emerged from McLellan's front door and were bunching up at the corner. An additional half-dozen bystanders had exited the Elks Club and were peering at the bank from the alley behind McLellan's. Things turned from bad to worse when a police siren started to wail and grew louder.

"Line 'em up!" Bentz yelled. Caroll and Fisher immediately began to pull the women up from the floor and the men followed.

Vera Correll swooned and fell into a heap. Gillis stood over her limp body screaming, "Get up, you bitch, get up!"

" Leave her!" Bentz commanded, and Gillis backed off.

A queue was formed next to the back door, and on Ed's "Go!" they were out and running. Bolt was first, followed by Gillis with the Thompson, then Welling, then Doyle huffing and puffing with a shotgun in one hand and a pistol in the other. Right behind came VanLopik and Pellegrom, with Caroll and Fisher staying close and brandishing their pistols. Lindemulder and Meschke were the final hostages, with Bentz bringing up the rear. Just before Martha stepped out the door Ed grabbed her around the waist and pulled her back inside. He gently pushed Martha behind the door, flashed her a smile, and stepped into the bright afternoon sun.

Tommy Caroll was yelling, "Car, car, car!" but Freddie and the Buick were nowhere to be seen. Instead, a black police cruiser appeared in the intersection and came to a screeching halt on the center line of Third Street. As the khaki-clad officers climbed out the passenger side of their vehicle a shotgun roared from the alcove at the side of McLellan's. Earl Doyle was hit in the head and chest with buckshot and reeled backward, dropping his shotgun. Caroll picked up the shotgun and returned fire. Additional shotgun blasts were now coming from the cover side of the police car as the sheriff's officers joined in with their riot guns. Welling dived for cover under a parked car and managed to avoid being hit. Pellegrom was hit in the foot by two pellets and stumbled to the pavement in the alley. VanLopik was hit in the neck and arm and lay writhing on the ground not far from Pellegrom. Lindemulder dived into some bushes and was grazed in the back as he went down.

Across Washington, on the steps of the post office building, a boy in short pants appeared to be shouting an Indian war-whoop at the top of his lungs as he hopped from one foot to the other with his arms held high. A well-dressed man in a dark suit and derby suddenly dashed out from the front door, snatched the child by the waist, and hauled him inside.

Caroll and Fisher were not hit and started to jog south toward Franklin. Each man carried a laundry bag of loot over his shoulder. Fisher repeatedly fired his pistol into the air to scare off would-be heroes.

As Bentz started to follow Caroll and Fisher he was hit twice in the lower back and almost knocked off his feet. His vest had stopped the bullets but it felt like he had been kicked in the kidneys by a mule. Bentz looked to his right and saw the shooter standing behind a Chevrolet convertible and taking aim again. Ed returned fire with his revolver and shot out the windshield of the Chevy. Bentz's adversary ducked out of sight as Ed squeezed off his last round. The deputies were now out from behind the patrol car and drawing their service revolvers as they advanced toward Bentz.

"Sorry, Verna old girl," Ed said grimly to himself. "Looks like I won't be home in time for supper."

The next instant, the space between the bank and the dime store erupted with a cacophony of machine gun fire, and the lawmen immediately retreated back to cover. The left front tire of the Nash was torn to shreds, the left doors were riddled, and the gas tank was punctured. In the middle of the street stood

Lester, laughing fiendishly as he sprayed the police car with bursts of hot lead. He held down the trigger of the Thompson as he pivoted to the left and tattooed a line at waist level down the brick wall of the McLellan store. Two slugs pierced the door in the alcove where Cotty Kinkema was kneeling, and knocked over a stack of watering cans inside the store.

With the trigger still down and the Thompson spitting a stream of bullets, Gillis continued to swivel his body to the left. The few bystanders remaining in the alley between McLellan's and the Elks Club started to scatter. As he turned to run, Captain Pleines was shot through the back and went down. The others, including Chuck Bugielski, were only spared because the Tommy gun jammed.

"C'mon Lester, let's make tracks!" screamed Big Ed. Gillis lowered the muzzle of the overheated submachine gun, took a split second to savor the carnage he had created, then turned to follow Bentz toward Franklin Street.

Earl Doyle had come to his senses and stared in disbelief as the rest of the troupe ran off. As he started to follow he was grabbed from behind by Ted Bolt. The two men struggled for Doyle's pistol and it went off, tearing away the webbing between the thumb and forefinger of Doyle's left hand. Screaming in pain, Doyle elbowed Bolt in the throat and the two men separated. Doyle started to point his pistol at Bolt's chest, but before Doyle could pull the trigger he was knocked off his feet by a tremendous blow to the temple. Cotty Kinkema, out of ammunition, had charged like a bellowing bull to his cousin's aid while swinging his shotgun like a club. The barrel caught Doyle along the side of his head and bowled him over. As Doyle went down, the heel and sole of his right shoe wedged between two pavers and the femur of his right leg snapped. Doyle screamed in agony for the second time and dropped his pistol. Bolt and Kinkema were on him like angry hounds. They dragged Doyle into the alley behind the bank and, as Will Pellegrom would later recount, "shook the bandit out of his clothes."

As Yetta Bonema's Chevrolet emerged from the driveway of Hatton Hospital and turned onto Franklin, her friend Emma

Miller thought she heard firecrackers in the distance. "Sounds like somebody's kids have Flashcrackas left over from the Fourth. My boys lighted all of theirs ten minutes after their father brought the things home - - against my wishes, I might add!" Both women giggled at the knuckle-headed behavior of married men.

As they approached the intersection with Third Street, a big fella in overalls stepped into the road waving his arms above his head. Yetta slammed on the brakes and the Miller boys whooped. In a flash the big man was at Yetta's window, but now he had a gun in his hand. "Get out!" he commanded.

A much shorter man, wearing a newsboy cap, appeared at Emma's window and shoved a gun barrel in her face. Mrs. Miller shrieked as he grabbed her arm and yelled, "Out!" Emma kicked her door open and the man yanked her out of the car and down to the sidewalk.

In the meantime, Yetta was being dragged from the driver's seat by the fellow in the overalls, tearing the shoulder strap of her house dress in the process. As Yetta fell to the pavement she screamed, "My baby, don't take my baby!"

The ruffian peered into the back seat to discover four wide-eyed children. He straightened up and yelled, "Get 'em out!" to a man wearing a straw hat, who now stood guard at the right rear door. A fourth man, wearing a fedora, was alongside the other suicide door. The straw hat quickly pulled the three Miller boys from their perch and out to the sidewalk, and then jumped into the back seat with a shotgun and a laundry bag in his lap. The fedora reached in from his side and lifted the kicking Barbara out of the car by her waist. As the portly man stood with the little girl at his eye level, she swung with all her might and caught him square in the mouth with her metal Mickey Mouse toy. He saw stars and lost hold of a bag that had been stuck under his arm. The little girl's sobbing mother snatched the child from the hoodlum's arms as he struggled to right himself. The dazed robber managed to remove his fedora before collapsing into the back seat, then leaned over and spit a broken tooth onto the pavement before slamming the car door shut.

The man in the overalls was now in the driver's seat and the little bandit was at his elbow. The little man drew a pistol from his belt, pointed it out the window towards Washington Street, and pulled the trigger three times as he shouted, "Go, go, go!"

✤

Chapter Seventeen

August 18, 1933

Bentz shoved the gear stick into first, popped the clutch and stomped on the gas, and the big Chevy leaped forward down Franklin. As the town armory came into view, Bentz hit the brakes and slammed the wheel to the left. The car took the corner on two wheels and roared up the steep hill that was Second Street.

At the top Bentz made another hairpin turn to the left and accelerated downhill on Lafayette Street. The road leveled out by the time he flew by the Boyden House and ran the stop sign at Fifth Street. By downshifting Bentz managed to negotiate

the three way junction where Lafayette merged into Pennoyer.
He swerved to miss a delivery truck that was backing into the
yard of Baker Lumber and clattered violently over some railroad
tracks.

Barely missing the opposite curb, Bentz hit the gas and
the Chevrolet flew eastward toward Highway 31. The stolen car
passed Ferry Elementary School doing at least fifty-five, while
boys on the sidewalk yelled their approval. Gillis grinned and
gave them a thumbs-up.

Turning south onto Highway 31, Bentz pushed the Chevy
to its limits. As the big sedan rocketed past Frieda Bierman's
farm the engine began to cough and lose power.

"Christ almighty!" cursed Gillis. "We're outta gas."

Bentz managed to steer the dying machine to the side of
the road next to a large hand-lettered sign that read *blueberries*.
Directly ahead, with the engine still running, sat a light blue
Chrysler Imperial with the top down. The driver's door was
open and a white-haired woman was sitting on the passenger's

side of the front seat, holding a little dog in her lap. The four robbers jumped from the Chevrolet and surrounded the Chrysler. Gillis stuck the end of the Thompson under the woman's nose and said, "Get out!" She froze.

A well-dressed man came running toward the blue car yelling, "Please, please don't hurt my wife, she's sick! Take my car and anything I have, but don't hurt her!"

Gillis turned and pointed the Tommy gun at the frantic husband. He stopped dead in his tracks. Stepping between Gillis and the petrified woman, Bentz opened her car door and offered his hand. Swallowing back tears, she took Bentz's arm and allowed him to walk her gingerly to her husband, the dog trotting obediently behind.

"Your wallet, please." The terrified man handed his wallet to Bentz, who removed three hundred dollars in cash and handed the empty billfold back to its owner.

Gillis, Fisher and Caroll were now in the Chrysler and Caroll was shouting, "Let's go, let's go!" Bentz tucked the cash into the front of his bibs, climbed into the driver's seat of the

Chrysler, and they were gone in a cloud of smoke and gravel.

Pursuers were not more than ten minutes behind the

escaping bandits. Within seconds after Doyle had been subdued,

Undersheriff Rycenga hopped into Bugielski's convertible and

called to Chuck to get in and drive south towards Holland.

About four miles south of town they were flagged down by a

very agitated older man who identified himself as Oscar Varneau

of Grand Rapids. Mr. Varneau quickly described how he had

been robbed at gunpoint and his Chrysler commandeered by four

rough men. Rycenga told Varneau to wait for the help that

would be along shortly, and then he and Bugielski roared off in

pursuit.

Only a few minutes behind Bugielski and Rycenga were

City Manager Pete Kammerad and Patrolman Ferdi Kinkema.

They caught up to Bugielski and Rycenga just south of Lake

Michigan Drive and the two vehicles pulled over so the men

could compare notes.

It was decided that Bugielski and Rycenga should search out a telephone in order to advise the Holland police to be on the lookout for the stolen Chrysler. Kammerad announced he was familiar with the woods and hills around the West Olive area, so he and Ferdi continued south to search the back roads in that locale.

Within an hour they discovered a Buick sedan abandoned in the woods along Pigeon Creek. Inside the car they found a Thompson submachine gun, several rifles, ammunition, cans of gasoline, roofing nails, medical supplies, maps and a handwritten log of driving directions. But the driver was nowhere to be found.

By nightfall West Olive was being combed by city police and deputies from several jurisdictions, the Michigan State Police, and a mob of armed citizens. A contingent of Coast Guardsmen from the *Escanaba* even set up Lewis machine guns in case the robbers returned for the Buick. After an all-night search, the posse was recalled. The bandits had made good their escape, with only hapless Earl Doyle left behind to face the music.

Chapter Eighteen

August 18 to December 6, 1933

Chief DeWitt returned from Ionia to an empty station house. The town was in an uproar. Ted Bolt and Mayor Lionel Heap quickly filled the Chief in on the melee that had exploded in his absence.

Nodding a "Thank you, gentlemen," DeWitt proceeded to spread a pile of current "wanted" circulars across his desk and asked Bolt to start reading the descriptions. Before long they came across an all-points bulletin issued by Collin County, Texas for "Edward W. Bents aka Edward W. Bentz". The wanted man's description seemed to match the big redheaded bandit who had been dressed in farmer's overalls, so DeWitt immediately

shot off a telegram to Texas requesting a photograph of Bentz.

As darkness fell, the mayor informed the Chief that the

sole captured bandit was under sedation at Hatton Hospital and

would not be worth an interrogation until the next day. With

nothing else to do, DeWitt loaded his sidearm and left to join the

search party at Pigeon River.

Earl Doyle recuperated at Hatton Hospital for three days

before being moved to the county jail on Tuesday morning. He

was arraigned in the afternoon. Carried into the courthouse on a

litter, Doyle was allowed to sit on top of a counsel table because

of his broken right leg. His injured left hand was bandaged and

he wore no socks or shoes. A handkerchief covered the wound

on his head, but he removed that cover when the judge entered

to take the bench.

Sheriff Rosema remained at Doyle's side and a well-

armed deputy stood immediately behind them. Doyle pleaded

"not guilty" to charges of robbery and assault with intent to commit murder but whispered to the sheriff that he would change his plea before trial.

Upon returning to his cell, Doyle was congenial to his jailers and friendly to reporters. He told the press, "I'm ready to take my medicine, but I won't squeal." Doyle steadfastly refused to name names.

A copy of Doyle's criminal record was provided by Hoover's Bureau of Investigation a week after the robbery. It showed Doyle to be a bootlegger, which he casually admitted was correct. He told everyone who would listen that the People's Bank job was his first armed robbery and that he sorely regretted becoming involved in such a dangerous and reckless plot. It was widely reported that Doyle would change his plea to "guilty" when the fall session of the circuit court opened for business in September.

It was also widely reported that the trial of Earl Doyle was to begin on Monday, September 11. The story was a ruse, planted by the sheriff and the county prosecutor. Doyle changed his plea during a secret court session held on Saturday afternoon,

September 9. He was immediately sentenced to life in prison by Circuit Judge Fred T. Miles. Early the next morning Doyle was spirited away to Jackson Prison by a heavily-armed guard comprised of the sheriff and his deputies and state police from the Grand Haven post. As the little convoy headed south, Doyle stared out the window and thought, "I'll miss my little Hazel, but I ain't gonna miss those damn Pekingese!"

Mug shots of Ed Bentz arrived from Texas during the first week of September. The Collin County sheriff also sent along mug shots of George Kelly, whom the Texas lawman identified as a "chum" of Bentz. Included with the mug shots of Ed Bentz and George Kelly were assorted pictures of persons labeled as Ed's "known associates and friends", including a picture of Ed's half-brother, Theodore. Ted Bolt immediately identified Ed Bentz as the big man in overalls who had cleaned out the People's Bank vault. Neither George Kelly nor the half-brother looked familiar to Bolt.

The next morning Bolt sent William Pellegrom, Vera Correll and John Lindemulder to the Chief's office to review photographs. Correll and Lindemulder could not identify anyone from the photographs. Pellegrom recognized Ed Bentz and "thought" that the half-brother looked familiar.

The conversation between DeWitt and Pellegrom was a bit strained because Pellegrom was hard of hearing and could not always tell if the Chief was saying "Ed" or "Ted". Later in the day, after the bank employees had gathered for their weekly staff meeting, Art Welling and Martha Meschke marched up the street to the police station to look at the Chief's pictures. They were adamant that both of the Bentzs had participated in the hold-up.

DeWitt then began a letter writing campaign that he would doggedly pursue for the next three years. Every time he read a news item or police flier describing a bank robbery that even remotely resembled the Grand Haven job in method or number of perpetrators, he would contact the authorities involved. DeWitt sent pictures of the Bentz brothers to police and sheriff departments in 18 states, Montreal, Canada, and even

Chatham, England. The Chief's request was always the same: "Do the Bentz brothers look familiar and if so where might they be found?"

The Grand Haven police tried to develop leads from the automobile discovered in the woods along the Pigeon River. It turned out that the Buick had been stolen from its rightful owner in Chicago by persons unknown. The sedan was turned over to an insurance adjuster on the same day that Doyle pled guilty. Doyle's pistol and shotgun and the firearms discovered in the Buick were also a dead end. Colt only had a record of the pistol's first delivery to a legitimate retailer, and Winchester only had similar records for the rifles. The Thompson's story was a bit more interesting. The exterior serial number had been removed, but the "secret" number placed on interior parts by the manufacturer revealed that the submachine gun had been sold to the Indiana National Guard in 1922. In the end, however, none of the weapons produced a good lead.

The next logical step was to follow the money. The cash and coin taken by the bandits were untraceable. The travelers checks, some issued by Mellon National Bank of Pittsburgh and the balance by American Express, were numbered and easily tracked. The checks started showing up by the end of September, first in Hammond, then in Milwaukee and Oshkosh. In each case the presenter signed his name "A.F. Krause". Chief DeWitt shared his photographs of the Bentz brothers with the investigators for Mellon Bank and Amex, and a few days thereafter Krause was tentatively identified as Theodore Bentz. Now standing and staring at the map of the United States that was hanging on his office wall, DeWitt thought, "The bastards are headed for St. Paul. It will be nigh impossible to flush them out of that rats' nest."

When DeWitt arrived at his office the next morning there was an excited buzz around City Hall. The evening headline of the September 26 *Grand Haven Daily Tribune* had screamed "Arrest 'Machine Gun' Kelly in Memphis". The accompanying story explained how George Kelly, wanted in several southern states for robbery and kidnapping, had been surprised in his sleep by Memphis police officers led by two of Hoover's special

agents. Kelly and his wife Kathryn had surrendered without a

fight to the "G-Men".

There were several copies of the story spread around the

police office at City Hall. The general consensus seemed to be

that when it came to notorious bandits like Kelly, the local

police did the footwork but Hoover's men always swooped in at

the last minute to grab the headlines. The Chief was not so

quick to condemn the federal men because he needed the

Bureau to provide a ballistics analysis for the weapons left

behind in West Olive. "Besides," DeWitt explained to his men,

"if Machine Gun Kelly ran with Ed Bentz in Texas it should not

be too hard to interest the G-Men in finding Bentz."

DeWitt immediately wrote a letter in longhand to J. E.

Hoover, in care of the U.S. Justice Department in Washington.

DeWitt informed Hoover that the Bentz brothers were wanted

in Grand Haven for bank robbery and that the getaway car had

been stolen in Illinois and crossed state lines. He closed his

letter by asking Hoover to "Wire collect any information you may receive in regard to the [Bentzs]." It took several days for one of the secretaries to type the letter, but it was in the mail by October 9.

By the end of October the trail of travelers checks turned back to the east. Checks were presented for payment in Toronto and in Montreal. Various names were used by the presenter, but he was always identified from photographs as Theodore Bentz. Bolstered by the unquestionable fact that Theodore Bentz was spending the stolen travelers checks, on November 3 the Chief sought and was granted an arrest warrant for Theodore Bentz.

The rest of November came and went without new developments in the case. The Chief started to worry that the trail had gone cold. Then, on an overcast December morning, his phone rang and the voice on the other end said in a soft Carolina drawl, "Good morning Chief, this is Special Agent Melvin Purvis of the Bureau of Investigation. Director Hoover has spoken with me about your efforts to catch Edward Bentz. How may I help?"

❧

WANTED FOR BANK ROBBERY.

EDWARD W. BENTZ, aliasNED DEWEY, JACK C. KEARNS, ARTHUR DESMOND. Age 38; Hgt. 5 ft. 11 in; Wt. 185; Eyes Blue; Hair Brown; Comp. Med. Dark; Occup. Mach. and Elect.; Born Minn.

It is requested that you hold anyone arrested with him until our witnesses arrive.

Wire collect,

D. B. Case # 5770

Detective Bureau,
Michigan State Police,
East Lansing, Michigan.
                    M.S.B. # 3948

E. "Ed" W. Bentz or Benz, aliases E. R. Richards, Ned Dewey, E. R. Ronaldson, etc.

Born North Dakota; age 37; medium build; height 5 feet 10½ inches; eyes blue-gray; hair brown; complexion medium; weight 170.

F. P. classification   13   Rr   18
                        ―   ―   ―
                        5   U

Albert L. Bates, aliases Albert Harris, James B. King, Bernard McLaughlin, etc.

Age 37; weight 170; height 5 feet 11 inches; build slim; hair light; eyes blue.

F. P. Classification :
                25   W   11   19
                26   U   10   17

Chief Lawrence DeWitt was able to collect several mug shots of Ed Bentz, which he used to prepare wanted bulletins. *Photographs courtesy of Grand Haven Department of Public Safety.*

PEOPLES SAVINGS BANK ROBBERY - August 18, 1933.

$100.00 REWARD

The American Express Company will pay a reward of One Hundred ($100.00) Dollars for information leading to the arrest and detention, until an officer arrives with papers, of THEODORE BENZ, whose photograph and description appears below. He has a criminal record, and is now a FUGITIVE FROM JUSTICE, being wanted on criminal charges by this Company, in numerous places.

F.P.C. 13 R: OO
23 -: M 20

DESCRIPTION

Age, 29 years, in 1933; Height, 5 feet, 11½ inches; Weight, 217 pounds; Light brown hair; Blue eyes.

Please transmit any information regarding BENZ by wire to either of the undersigned.

D. E. RICHER, Inspector,
American Express Company,
65 Broadway, New York City.
Phone: WHitehall 4-2000

G. B. PLOWMAN, Special Agent,
American Express Company,
58 E. Washington St., Chicago, Illinois
Phone: FRAnklin 6565

Chicago, Ills. October 5, 1933

The detectives of the American Express Company were instrumental in pursuing the paper trail left behind by Teddie Bentz. *Photographs courtesy of Grand Haven Department of Public Safety.*

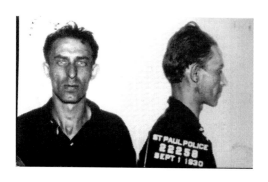

Tommy Caroll (22258) and Chuck Fisher (23977) pulled jobs together in St. Paul before joining up with Lester Gillis. The picture of Earl Doyle shows him swathed in bandages after his capture. *Photographs courtesy of Grand Haven Department of Public Safety.*

During his investigation of the People's Bank robbery, Chief Lawrence DeWitt collected dozens of mug shots of known bank robbers, including a photograph of "George Nelson". No witness ever identified Nelson (Lester Gillis) as the little robber with the Thompson submachine gun. *Photographs courtesy of Grand Haven Department of Public Safety.*

The Sky Ride was the premier attraction of the 1933 World's Fair. This view shows the east tower, located on Northerly Island. *Photograph courtesy of The University of Chicago Library, digital collection for A Century of Progress.*

This view, possibly taken from a blimp, shows the enclosed lower observation deck and open upper observation deck of a Sky Ride tower. *Photograph courtesy of The University of Chicago Library.*

This double exposure shows a woman peering north from the open upper observation deck. *Photograph courtesy of the University of California caliphere collection.*

By 2010 most of the uninsulated seasonal cottages in Long Beach, such as "Sleepy Nest", had been torn down to make room for year-round homes. Only a few of the seasonal variety remain. This cottage is an example of the survivors. The enclosed porch and steps face the beach. On the opposite side is a driveway that climbs up to the grade of Lake Shore Drive. *Photograph courtesy of Bartleby and Me, LLC.*

As of 2010, Belle Casa still stands on a hill above Lake Shore Drive. The home has had several owners since 1933, all of whom were connected in some way to Chicago politics. One of the title transfers resulted from the luxury cottage being lost in a card game. The current owner graciously allowed the author to spend a long summer weekend at the home while finishing the manuscript of this story. *Photograph courtesy of Bartleby and Me, LLC.*

Lindemulder, Correll, Bolt, Meschke and Pellegrom posed for this front page shot the day after the robbery. Photograph courtesy of *The Grand Haven Tribune*.

Interior photographs of People's Bank were staged in 1934 as demonstrative trial exhibits. Photographs courtesy of *The Grand Haven Tribune.*

Freddie Monahan abandoned the troupe's stolen Buick in the woods near Port Sheldon. Inside the police found a Thompson submachine gun, rifles, ammunition, and a detailed description of the "get". The car was returned to its rightful owner in Chicago. *Photograph courtesy of Grand Haven Department of Public Safety.*

Business as Usual

DEPRESSIONS come and go,
BANK HOLIDAYS come to an end,
BANK HOLDUPS occur,

But Business Goes on As Usual at

The Peoples Savings Bank

"The Bank Where You Feel at Home"

A State Bank—Member Federal Reserve System

People's Bank was not about to let a gang of Chicago hoodlums impede business! The directors of the bank ran this advertisement in the local paper just five days after the robbery. Image courtesy of *The Grand Haven Tribune*.

This 2010 photograph shows Ottawa County Sheriff Gary Rosema, grand-nephew of Sheriff Ben Rosema, holding the Tommy gun recovered from the getaway car that was abandoned by Freddy Monahan in Port Sheldon. The Thompson has been maintained in working condition in the Sheriff Department's evidence locker since 1933. *Photograph taken by the Hon. Edward R. Post, Ottawa County Circuit Court Judge.*

Chapter Nineteen

January 1 to July 16, 1934

After the New Year, DeWitt renewed his letter-writing campaign to police departments across the Midwest. He hired Pippel Printing to prepare a circular with mug shots of Ed and Theodore Bentz and Earl Doyle, and a description of the Grand Haven robbery. Also included was a list of the travelers checks and railroad bonds that were still missing. A copy of the circular was shared with other police departments at every opportunity. Every so often the Chief would receive a reply, but no leads.

Every small town has its loudmouths and Grand Haven was no different. On a weekly basis the Chief had to endure some smart alec comment about his absence from town on the day of the People's Bank robbery, or about his dogged but so far unsuccessful pursuit of the Bentz brothers. When responding to a prowler complaint at the home of a prominent businessman, DeWitt was greeted by the lady of the house as "our own Inspector Javert". The literary reference was explained to the Chief by his daughter that night at supper. He winced but said nothing.

The weather warmed into spring but the trail of the Bentz brothers just grew colder. On May 23, DeWitt opened the *Tribune* to a headline of "Clyde Barrow, Bonnie Parker Are Killed." The reporter explained how the lovers-turned-killers died in a hail of bullets on a country road in Louisiana. They had been hunted down by a combined posse of Texas and Louisiana lawmen led by the famous Texas Ranger Frank Hamer.

The next morning DeWitt spoke with Special Agent Purvis by telephone. The two men had become friends as they worked the Bentz case. Purvis was the only other lawman who still gave DeWitt encouragement in his one-man manhunt, which the Chief deeply appreciated. DeWitt had come to realize that Purvis was a lawyer with no real police experience, but the Chief never thought less of the younger man for it. Sometimes Purvis asked the Chief for advice about routine arrest and interrogation procedures, and the veteran cop did his best to help. That morning their conversation began with an almost jovial exchange about Bonnie and Clyde.

"Melvin, it appears Frank Hamer finally caught up to Clyde Barrow and his moll."

"Yes sir, it's all over the papers and on the radio. Director Hoover attempted to contact Mr. Hamer to offer the Bureau's congratulations, but the Ranger was otherwise disposed at a saloon and could not be bothered to come to the telephone."

DeWitt chuckled and then his tone became serious. "Melvin, everybody knows them Texas Rangers, Hamer especially, don't fool around. If a man's wanted for serious crimes and is a known killer, the Rangers shoot first and ask questions later."

"I know," Purvis replied.

The Chief continued, "You and your men are a new breed, with new methods, and I respect that. To catch a crook like Ed Bentz takes perseverance and finesse, and you college boys at the Bureau have plenty of both. Just remember that the young toughs you are after have plenty of teeth and are not afraid to bite."

"You mean Dillinger - - and Floyd?"

"Damn right I do. When you catch up to them don't play around. Just ask yourself what would old Frank Hamer do. And be careful!"

"Chief DeWitt, I will, as always, defer to your experience in such matters." Purvis gave a warm goodbye and the line went dead.

On June 8 the *Tribune* briefly reported that a "Dillinger Aide" had been shot and killed by police in Waterloo, Iowa. Chief

DeWitt gave the news item short shrift as the name Tommy Caroll meant nothing to him.

DeWitt picked up the Bentz brothers' trail again the day after he spoke to Purvis. DeWitt was notified by Mellon National Bank that one of the stolen travelers checks had been used on May 28 to buy tires in a little Massachusetts town on the border with New Hampshire. The Chief immediately sent his circular about the Bentz brothers to the local police, and they replied that the buyer of the tires had been positively identified as Theodore Bentz. Bentz had been driving a taxicab and had loaded the tires into the back seat and trunk before driving off. A few weeks later DeWitt learned that the taxi had been stolen at gunpoint, and both of the Bentz brothers had been identified as the carjackers.

During his follow-up telephone conversations with local police in Massachusetts and Vermont, Chief DeWitt learned that a bank robbery had occurred in Danville, Vermont on June 4. The Chief sent pictures of Ed and Theodore Bentz to the banker in Danville, who in turn passed them on to Vermont States

Attorney Sterry Waterman and to the Special Agent in charge of

the Boston office of the Bureau of Investigation. Waterman

promptly called DeWitt to thank him for the pictures and to

congratulate him for helping to crack the Danville case.

"Beg pardon, Mr. Waterman, but just how did I do that?"

DeWitt was puzzled.

"Well, Chief, our local sheriff just happened to have one

of your circulars about the Bentz brothers on his desk, and when

it was shown to the bank employees Ed Bentz was positively

identified as one of the robbers." Waterman's tone was almost

giddy.

"What about Theodore?" asked DeWitt.

"Nobody can place him inside the bank, so for now we are

presuming he was the wheel man waiting outside in the stolen

taxi."

"That explains why he bought new tires."

"I totally agree. Thanks to you, Chief, we knew right away

who to look for. An all-points bulletin is covering New England.

The jig will soon be up for the Bentz brothers. When we catch 'em maybe you and I can 'split the take' – I'll try one and you can have the other!"

"Sounds good," was all the Chief could get out.

"I must leave you now as I am late for a meeting. If possible please send me a list of the checks and bonds stolen from your bank in Grand Haven and we will keep an eye out for them. Good job, sir, first rate!"

The call ended and the Chief sat in his chair dumbfounded for several minutes before realizing that he needed to cradle the receiver.

The grass outside City Hall was still wet with morning dew when the Western Union delivery boy came bounding up the stairs to the Chief's office two at a time. The youngster had ridden his bicycle as fast as it would take him from the telegraph office at the bottom of Washington to City Hall at the top of the hill. He now stood at attention in front of Chief DeWitt's desk, breathing heavily but grinning from ear to ear, and held out the envelope as if it contained Lee's surrender.

"Boss said take this to the Chief pronto, it will make his day."

The chief reached into his pocket for his new glasses and opened the envelope. The pasted lines of the telegram read:

JOHNSBURY VT   1934 JUL 16   AM 7 33

LAWRENCE DEWITT =

CHIEF OF POLICE GRAND HAVEN MICH =

THEODORE BENTZ IN CUSTODY PORTLAND MAINE

FEDERAL AUTHORITIES

SINCERELY =

STERRY R WATERMAN STATES ATTORNEY.

When DeWitt looked up, his office was overflowing with City employees, all holding their breath. He stood slowly and walked to the bulletin board where he very deliberately pinned

the telegram over a copy of the wanted circular for the Bentzs.
He turned to face the little crowd.

"We need to send a copy of our arrest warrant for
Theodore Bentz to the U.S. Attorney in Portland, Maine. And
somebody please get Dethmers on the line so he can get started
on papers for extradition."

The room burst into cheers.

Chapter Twenty

July 22 & 23, 1934

John Dillinger was ambushed by Melvin Purvis' men on the humid evening of Sunday, July 22. The good-looking Indiana farm boy had become a national celebrity in the year since he had broken bread with Ed Bentz at the Karpis cottage. Time and again Dillinger had bested state and federal authorities, with a trail of dead bodies to show for it. The level of violence in a Dillinger robbery had increased several fold after Johnnie had joined forces with Lester Gillis in March. It was almost impossible to rein in the little man once the shooting started.

"Bullets End Dillinger's Crime Career," screamed the July 23 edition of the *Grand Haven DailyTribune*. It was all anyone wanted to talk about at City Hall, so very little work got done that Monday. Late that evening, at home, Lawrence DeWitt was awakened from a deep sleep by the insistent ring of his bedside telephone. The Chief sat up, cleared his throat, and said, "Hello, DeWitt here." It was Melvin Purvis on the line.

"Well, Chief, I got my man," said Purvis slowly. His voice was heavy and lacked its characteristic charm. Over the last several months the two lawmen had spoken many times, but never this late at night. DeWitt wondered if the Agent had been drinking.

"I know, read it in the paper. Good work, Special Agent." Purvis let out a long sigh on the other end but said nothing. The Chief continued.

"I'm close to getting my man as well. Six weeks ago the Bentzs held up a little bank in Vermont. The Portland police picked up Ted Bentz and are holding him on order of the US Attorney. Apparently Mr. Theodore has come up with a good alibi for the Vermont heist, so hopefully my request for his extradition back to Grand Haven will be granted. Your boys in Boston are still looking for Ed. Before the year is up I may have the satisfaction of seeing both those sons-of-bitches locked up for good."

"Chief," Purvis interrupted, "you ever order an assassination?" DeWitt thought he heard the agent choke back a sob. The Chief waited until there was steady breathing on the other end before answering.

"No, Melvin, I can't say that I have."

"It is not . . ." Purvis was searching for the word, " . . . honorable. I feel like a murderer of the basest kind."

DeWitt lowered his voice and said, "Now you listen to me. During the War I did things that I am not proud of. But they needed to be done, for the greater good. John Dillinger was a menace to every decent man and woman. So put down your bottle and get some sleep. We will talk again soon . . . son."

Try as he might the Chief could not get back to sleep, so he dressed and drove to the station to check on his men.

Chapter Twenty One

February 15 to July 28, 1934

Since the middle of February Ed and Verna Bentz had been living in Portland, Maine as "Mr. and Mrs. Frederick Wendell." They rented a furnished house in the nicest part of town and Ed started a legitimate toy wholesale business. Teddy arrived in early April and went to work at the toy company under the alias "Theodore Craig". Ed had grown a bushy moustache and nobody but Verna knew the two men were brothers.

Ed was on the road selling night and day, but by the end of May his toy company was starting to founder. During a sales run to Manchester and Burlington Ed drove by a little bank in Danville, Vermont that looked like the sort of place where he could do business. On June 4, Bentz and an accomplice made a forced withdrawal of almost five thousand dollars. The money helped keep the toy company afloat for awhile, but soon after the robbery the mysterious Mr. Wendell became a person of interest to the Portland police. Ed could tell that his house was being watched during the day, so late one rainy night he packed a bag and headed for Albany.

As Ed backed his car from the garage Verna ran out to him with one hand at the collar of her robe and the other holding a thermos of hot coffee. "Sell all the furniture as quick as you can and take the train to your mother's house in Milwaukee," he said. "I'll send for you when the coast is clear."

Verna did not let herself cry until the tail lights of Ed's car disappeared in the rain. She was soaked by the time she went back in the house.

◊ ◊ ◊

The policeman in charge of surveillance at the Wendell house was Harold "Mac" Maguire, a third-generation member of the Portland police department. Maguire's father and grandfather had walked the beat on every street, back alley and dock of the old port city. Mac, to the immense pride of his father, earned a gold detective's shield when he was only twenty-five years old. Two decades had come and gone and now Mac was Sergeant Maguire, grizzled veteran of detectives. He looked the part: tall and rangy, with almost no hair left to comb under his dented fedora. Maguire's dusty shoes had holes in their soles and his suit was forever in need of a good pressing. He carried a thirty-two caliber Colt Detective Special in his right coat pocket and a pair of handcuffs and a small knife in the left. In twenty-six years on the force he had never fired a shot in anger.

In addition to watching the Wendell house, Maguire made more than a half dozen trips to the toy company where Wendell supposedly worked. The detective never was able to catch up to Wendell for a face-to-face, but during his last visit Mac managed to have pleasant conversation with the company's manager, Ted

Craig. Mr. Craig explained that Wendell worked for the company
as head of sales and, "In these trying times he is on the road
every waking moment trying to drum up business."

The two men shared fly fishing stories for an hour until
Craig opined that Wendell probably would not be calling in to the
office that day. Craig gave Maguire some toys for his grandkids
and promised to send Wendell by the police station when the
salesman returned from his current trip to Lowell, Albany and
Rutland.

On July 15, Maguire's chief asked him to sit in on a
meeting with United States Attorney John Thompson of the
Justice Department's Portland office, Special Agent McCean of
the Bureau's Boston office and police officers from Vermont and
Massachusetts. The topic of discussion was the Danville bank
job.

"Oh, wonderful," thought Mac, "another useless meeting
and a big waste of my time." But his boss said go, so he went.

After introductions were made, Attorney Thompson
started the meeting by removing pictures of Edward Bentz and

Theodore Bentz from his briefcase and passing them around the table. Maguire was treated as the junior man, so the pictures came to him last.

"These men are brothers," Thompson began, "and are wanted in Michigan for..." He was not able to finish because of an outburst from Maguire.

"Hot damn, I know one of these guys – Theodore Bentz – he works right here in Portland! Calls himself Ted Craig."

Thompson looked dubious. "Are you sure of this, Detective?"

"As sure as I know Mrs. Maguire will serve cod on Friday. I can get up from this table and have Craig . . . er, Bentz . . . under arrest in ten minutes."

"OK," Thompson smiled, "let's see you do it."

Ted Bentz had just got off the phone with Verna. She told him that Ed had left for "a very long trip" and that Verna would shortly follow. Verna told Teddy that Ed wanted him to discount and collect as many receivables as possible in the next

three days, keep the cash, and walk away from the warehouse.
Ted wished his sister-in-law "good luck" and drained his coffee
cup. He was about to get up for a refill when his office door
swung open to reveal Sergeant Maguire standing alone with a
hand in his right coat pocket.

"What's the trouble, Mac?" asked Teddy.

"You know what the trouble is: you're under arrest, so
come along."

Ted stood up and turned around with his hands behind
his back. The big detective slapped on the cuffs, grabbed
Teddy's coat and hat from the rack in the corner and led Bentz
by the arm down the stairs and out the door to a waiting cruiser.
Teddy was booked at the station house as Ted Craig. Maguire's
trip to and from the toy company had been accomplished in just
under twenty minutes.

The case against Theodore Craig aka Theodore Bentz for
the Danville bank job was not going well for United States
Attorney Thompson. The bank employees had no problem

identifying Ed Bentz as the robber, even though he was clean-shaven in his mug shot. They could not make the same positive identification of Craig. To make matters worse, Craig's attorney had given notice of several alibi witnesses who would put Craig in Portland at the time of the Danville holdup. Special Agent McCean and Detective Maguire interviewed those witnesses and reported back to Thompson that they were very credible.

Thompson told his officers that the federal case against Craig would most likely be dismissed at the July 28 preliminary hearing. McCean passed the bad news on to his counterpart in Chicago. Purvis immediately called Chief DeWitt and told him that Ted Bentz would probably be released from federal custody in two days but could be immediately arrested on the Michigan charges if the Chief cared to make the trip to Portland. DeWitt thanked his young friend very much, hung up the phone and walked over to the jail to speak with Sheriff Rosema.

The federal courthouse in Portland was built in 1911 in the Italian Renaissance Revival style. Two stories tall and entirely faced in Vermont granite, its trapezoidal footprint covers an entire city block. The main entrance is located at the angled corner of Federal and Market streets, and is enshrined by a triangular pediment above a Doric frieze. It was from this ostentatious portal that Mr. and Mrs. Theodore Bentz emerged into the warm sunshine just before noon on July 28. The federal charge against Teddy for robbery of the Danville bank had just been dropped due to 'insufficient evidence'. Waiting at the curb to meet them was Sergeant Mac Maguire.

"Well hello, Mac," grinned Teddy. "Nice day to be out for a stroll, don't you think?" Bentz nodded to his wife and said, "Mac, this is my wife Catherine. Catherine, this is my good friend Sergeant Mac."

Maguire nodded and said, "Nice to make your acquaintance." Mac then gently removed Catherine's hand from Teddy's arm and replaced it with his viselike grip. With his other hand Maguire pulled handcuffs from his pocket and pointed with them to the other side of the street.

"Ted, I have some friends who want very much to meet you." Across the narrow intersection, standing shoulder to shoulder in dress uniform, were Grand Haven Police Chief Lawrence DeWitt and Ottawa County Sheriff Benjamin Rosema.

Chapter Twenty Two

July 29 to September 25, 1934

On the trip back to Grand Haven Ted Bentz admitted that he had cashed traveler's checks stolen from People's Bank by his brother Ed, but he steadfastly denied that he participated in the robbery, saying "My brother did not want me anywhere near his 'big job', and he gave me some of the traveler's checks because he owed me money."

Ted went on to explain how Ed had decided to "go straight" with the Portland toy company, which in turn had provided Teddy with a new job and a fresh start. Furthermore, Ted insisted that he was in his Chicago apartment at 7905 Luella

Avenue on the day of the robbery, which could be proven from pick-up records maintained by his dry cleaner.

The Chief politely listened but at the end of the story told Bentz to, "save it for the jury." When Ted tried to find a sympathetic ear with Ben Rosema, the sheriff just cut him short with a "Don't bother."

A week after his return to Grand Haven, DeWitt drove to the shop of Ted's Chicago dry cleaner and examined the pick-up log. There were entries for 'T. Craig' on August 17, 21 and 24, 1933, but nothing for August 18. The Chief reported his findings to County Prosecutor John Dethmers. The prosecutor was up for re-election and his campaign ad ran in the paper alongside the stories about Bentz's capture and extradition back to Grand Haven. Dethmers decided that DeWitt need not spend any more of the taxpayers' money trying to dig up alibi witnesses for Bentz. The accused could find them on his own nickel.

Catherine Bentz had followed her husband back to Grand Haven. During a jail visit on August 13, Teddy gave Catherine his handwritten notes about persons who could be contacted in

Michigan City and Chicago to establish Teddy's whereabouts on

August 18, 1933. Those notes were reviewed by the Sheriff's

Office but no effort was made by the prosecution to interview

any of the people on Bentz's list.

The preliminary examination for Teddy's case took place

on August 22 and 23 before Circuit Court Commissioner Daniel

Pagelsen. Prosecutor John Dethmers appeared for the People

and Attorney Louis Osterhous for the defendant.

Will Pellegrom was the prosecution's star witness to

identify Teddy. Pellegrom knew that Teddy and Doyle were not

the same robber because Pellegrom had watched Doyle get

beaten to a pulp by Ted Bolt and Ed Kinkema. He likewise had a

good recollection of the small man with the machine gun,

although no one in the court room realized that robber was

Lester Gillis aka Baby Face Nelson. Pellegrom also was adamant

that Teddy was not the big redheaded fellow dressed in overalls.

Will remained steadfast that even though he had only

briefly observed Teddy from a distance of more than six feet, and

only through the bars of the teller cages, Bentz was one of the robbers and had definitely worn a white straw hat. The commissioner found sufficient cause to bind Theodore Bentz over for trial and set bond at twenty-five thousand dollars.

By the time Teddy's circuit court arraignment went forward on Thursday, September 20, he and Catherine had run out of money to pay lawyers. She had spent the last of their savings to pay a private detective to locate alibi witnesses in Chicago. Attorney Osterhous appeared on Teddy's behalf for the last time and Attorney Elbern Parsons was appointed *in absentia* to represent Bentz, at public expense, as trial counsel. Trial in the case of *The People of the State of Michigan v Theodore Bentz* was scheduled to commence the following Monday, September 24. Ted Bentz would face the jury with defense counsel he would meet just once before opening statements.

For two days Prosecutor John Dethmers and defense counsel Elbern Parsons sparred inside the Romanesque brick courthouse that overlooked downtown Grand Haven. Eight witnesses testified for the prosecution and six for the defense.

Parsons never made a motion to sequester the prosecution witnesses.

To begin the prosecution's case Will Pellegrom was called to repeat his identification testimony from the preliminary examination. Parsons was not able to shake Will's confidence during cross-examination. Martha Meschke and Art Welling also testified that they thought Theodore was present during the robbery with his brother Edward, and Parsons did not press them very much.

Ted Bolt testified that he could not identify any of the robbers other than Earl Doyle, Ed Bentz and the unidentified "little fellow with the machine gun". John Lindemulder followed Bolt's lead when it came to identifying bandits and, like Pellegrom, testified that only four gunmen had entered the bank on the day of the robbery.

The prosecution called a shopkeeper from Hammond, Indiana who testified that Teddy had bought a hat with one of the traveler's checks. Chief Lawrence DeWitt took the stand to repeat Teddy's "confession" about how he had received the travelers checks from his brother Ed. Guilt by association was the meat of the prosecution's case.

After the prosecution rested, Attorney Parsons presented four alibi witnesses. Those witnesses were sequestered because the prosecutor made the effort to ask for their separation. The first witness for the defense was Lonnie Bailey, a Negro janitor in the Chicago building where Ted and Catherine had rented a tourist apartment a year earlier. Bailey testified that he had entered the Bentzs' space on the afternoon of August 18 to clean the floors. He recalled that both Ted and Catherine were home at the time.

Under cross examination the prosecutor suggested that the "colored boy" had actually worked in the Bentz apartment a week *before* August 18. Bailey held his ground and calmly stated that the payroll records kept by his employer could confirm his recollection of the date. Unfortunately Attorney Parsons had not obtained those records for evidence.

The second alibi witness was Aaron Shugan, a druggist who operated a shop in the same building that contained the

Bentzs' apartment. He was certain that Ted Bentz had been in his shop on the afternoon of August 18 to buy medicine for his wife. However, the druggist could not produce a counter prescription as evidence of the sale.

The third alibi witness was Shugan's assistant, who backed up his employer's story so completely that a cynic might conclude the two men had rehearsed their testimony.

Earl Doyle was up next. He had been transported to Grand Haven from Jackson prison for the day and was thoroughly enjoying his time "on the outside". Parsons had Teddy stand, then asked Doyle if the defendant was one of Doyle's "associates" on the day of the robbery.

Doyle replied, "He was not."

On cross exam Doyle steadfastly refused to name any of the other members of the troupe. He ended his testimony by admitting that he was a convicted felon serving a life sentence in the penitentiary. Attorney Parsons decided to end the first day of defense testimony on that low note.

◇ ◇ ◇

The second day of trial began with Catherine Bentz giving evidence for her husband. She explained that Teddy and she had driven to Chicago from British Columbia in August of 1933, and had taken up temporary residence in a tourist apartment next to the drug store on August 16.

She explained that they had come to Chicago for the express purpose of visiting the World's Fair, and that's why they had rented a short-term apartment. She corroborated the testimony given by Bailey and Shugan.

Dethmers began Catherine's cross-examination by making her admit that in August of 1933 she was cohabiting with Ted without the benefit of a marriage license. Catherine tearfully insisted that she and Ted were eventually married in November of 1933, but the damage to her reputation and credibility had been done.

For reasons unknown, neither the prosecution nor the defense called Yetta Bonema or Emma Miller as witnesses.

Theodore Bentz exercised his Fifth Amendment right to not take the stand in his own defense.

In reaction to the rising tide of lawlessness during the Great Depression, in 1931 the Michigan Legislature had approved life imprisonment as the maximum penalty for bank robbery. Circuit Judge Fred T. Miles began his charge to the all-male jury by reading the statute aloud:

> "Any person who, with intent to commit the crime of larceny shall confine, maim, injure or wound or put in fear any person for the purpose of stealing from any bank, or shall by intimidation, fear or threats compel any person to disclose or surrender the means of opening any vault shall, whether he succeeds or fails in the perpetration of such larceny, be guilty of a felony, *punishable by imprisonment in the state prison for life* or any term of years."

Judge Miles then explained to the jurors that there were two elements to be proved against the defendant: Did an armed robbery of People's Bank take place on August 18, 1933, and did Theodore Bentz participate as one of the robbers?

The judge instructed the jurors that the first element had been proved beyond all doubt, so they were to focus on the question of whether or not Theodore Bentz was present during the robbery. Miles then briefly summed up the evidence offered by both sides. Judge Miles wrapped up his charge to the jury in less than five minutes and the panel was led away by the bailiff to deliberate.

While the jury was out, Dethmers and Parsons retired to the lawyers' lounge for a smoke. Dethmers offered Parsons a light and quipped, "Elbern, don't worry so much about Fred throwing the book at your man. If Bentz is not guilty of this hold-up, he sure as hell is guilty of something just like it, or worse, somewhere else!"

The jury was out for barely two hours. They found Ted guilty as charged. Parsons did not ask for each juror to be polled on whether or not he agreed with the verdict. Teddy asked if he could address the jury before he was sentenced, and the judge allowed it.

"What I have got to say is that I am innocent of this offense and it will be on your conscience, boys, all your lives. I never robbed this bank, and it will be proven sooner or later. That is all I have to say."

Judge Miles then passed sentence. "The sentence of this court is that you be imprisoned in the Michigan State Prison at Marquette during the remainder of your life." He turned to the jurors and thanked them for their service, saying, "You did the right thing. After the testimony was in, from the information that was presented to me as to the history of this man, you need not worry at all about the possibility of Theodore Bentz being not guilty."

❧

Chapter Twenty Three

August 18 & 19, 1933

The troupe was only halfway to Allegan when the growing pain in Ed's lower back forced him to pull over and let Lester drive. A great contusion had swelled in the small of Ed's back where, apparently, his vest had stopped two thirty-eight rounds. The pain was excruciating when Bentz attempted to depress the brake and clutch pedals. After trading places with Lester, Ed turned on his side and rode along on one cheek.

Gillis was by nature a maniac behind the wheel. He pushed the big Chrysler to its limits, barely slowing down for bumps and ruts, which evoked a steady stream of curses from the three passengers. As the foursome motored through Marshall the mood turned even more sour when Caroll realized that one of the loot bags had been left behind because Fisher had been hit in the mouth by a little girl. In no uncertain terms, Caroll offered to knock out the rest of Fisher's front teeth. Fisher, nursing a split lip and a mouthful of dried blood, was in no mood to be the subject of ridicule. They would have come to blows but for the need to hold on to their seats while Lester was at the wheel.

After three-and-a-half hours of hard driving, the bandits had covered one hundred seventy miles of gravel and blacktop and reached the rolling hills just north of the small farm town of Hudson, Michigan. As they rounded a curve in the dimming daylight, the road was unexpectedly blocked by a wayward Guernsey. Gillis turned the wheel violently to avoid the steadfast bovine, and the right front tire blew with a loud pop. The Chrysler pitched headlong into the ditch, shearing off a headlamp and running the radiator onto the protruding limb of a small pignut hickory. The travelers were tossed about violently, but nobody was thrown from the vehicle.

Gillis and Fisher climbed out of the wrecked automobile first, followed by Caroll. All three helped pull Bentz slowly out of the front seat. He was able to stand and walk about, though slowly. Without conversation all four men inspected the damage. Finally Bentz broke the silence.

"We are afoot now, boys. Before it becomes completely dark, let's gather our things and split the take." With that, they knelt in a circle at the side of the road and emptied the contents of the two remaining laundry bags into a pile. The count was just over thirty-five hundred dollars in cash, six thousand dollars in traveler's checks issued by American Express and Mellon National Bank, and seven long-term income bonds issued by the Chicago, St. Paul & Milwaukee Railroad. It was not the haul they had hoped for.

"Son of a bitch!" Fisher lisped painfully through swollen lips.

"Can't believe we almost bought the farm for this," agreed Caroll.

"I've had better days," confessed Big Ed.

In contrast, Gillis was almost giddy about the outcome of his first well-organized heist. "We showed them small town coppers who's boss! The next job will be a cinch. An' I say that yellow bastard Freddie don't get no share!" He smiled at Bentz and asked, "Maybe Doyle won't need his share either?"

"Hazel gets Earl's full share, and that's a fact." Ed's stern pronouncement made Lester zip his lip.

"I never spent no traveler's checks before," interjected Caroll. " Not sure I want to. And I sure as hell don't want to peddle no railroad papers!" Fisher nodded his head in mute agreement.

Bentz quickly did the numbers in his head and announced, "Tell you what we'll do. Each of you boys take eight hundred seventy-five dollars in cash and one thousand three hundred seventy dollars in traveler's checks. I'll explain how to use the checks later. Hazel gets the same amount of cash and checks. Teddy will be paid his half-share in traveler's checks, which will be one thousand one hundred twenty dollars. For my share, I will keep the railroad bonds because I know a fence who will take them off my hands." He looked around the small circle for a hint of dissent but found none. "OK then, let's count it out and get down the road before some hayseed who drives worse than Lester runs us over."

After dividing the loot, the troupe walked in silence for about fifteen minutes before coming upon a Ford Model A panel truck that was pulled over to the shoulder. "Fayette Farms" was emblazoned in gold and black block letters on the sides and rear of the truck, and an Ohio license plate was bolted to the back bumper. The young driver and his two passengers were down in the ditch relieving themselves.

"There's our ride home," said Bentz in a low voice to Gillis. Ed waved to the startled trucker with one big hand while nonchalantly reaching for his thirty-eight with the other.

◊ ◊ ◊

It was a slow, monotonous drive back to Long Beach. The panel truck had bald tires, so they kept the speed at or below forty mph. When back spasms made Ed vomit out the passenger window they pulled over at a truck stop and bought some shaved ice and two mechanic's towels. From those basics Ed made cold compresses which he held to the small of his back. Thankfully the swelling seemed to go down a bit, and after awhile Bentz drifted in and out of a light sleep while propped up against the front passenger door. In the meantime, Gillis and Caroll took turns driving while Fisher stretched out on the floor of the storage compartment and snored his way back to Indiana.

Verna was sitting in the kitchen clothed in a robe and nightdress when Ed eased his way up the back steps of Sleepy Nest at 5 a.m. on Saturday morning. Unable to fall asleep in bed, after midnight she had moved downstairs and napped for a few hours in one of the front-room chairs. At 4 a.m. Verna had jolted awake as if from a bad dream, gathered herself and went into the kitchen to light a fire and make tea. She was sitting quietly with her cup, misty-eyed, when her man finally walked through the door and into her arms.

It had taken less than a half hour for Ed to recount the high and low points of the Grand Haven job and to share the very bad news that bystanders had been shot and Doyle had been captured. After washing down a handful of aspirin with a small single malt, Ed collapsed and slept for almost eight hours.

When Bentz awakened, he was able to stand without too much difficulty, so he bathed, shaved and headed downstairs to where Verna was putting a cherry pie in the oven and tending a pot of pea soup.

"Well, look who's up among the living," said Verna as she stood on tiptoes to kiss Ed's smooth chin. "Go sit in the front room and I'll bring you some lemonade from the ice box." He did as he was told. The well-cushioned chair felt good against his sore back.

"Have you seen Hazel?" he called back to the kitchen.

"Oh, yes," Verna answered. "She's a mess. Helen and I did our best to convince her that it's too risky to contact Earl right now. Lester says Earl is 'old school' and will never rat on anybody, but the police might try to jam him up by charging Hazel as an accomplice. Hazel didn't want to hear any of it; just sat there on Helen's glider bawling and squeezing one of her snuffly little dogs. I think she'd make a beeline for Grand Haven if she could drive."

"Good thing she can't, then," Ed offered.

Verna entered the room with a pitcher of lemonade, two glasses of ice, and a plate of ginger snaps. "Teddy and Catherine left yesterday before lunch. Catherine was throwing up all morning. I wonder if Teddy knows what that means?"

"It means now he *really* should marry the girl." Ed sipped at his drink and tried to find a posture that would take the pressure off his lower back.

"So now what?"

"We can't stay in Long Beach. Doyle may be 'old school', but sooner or later the cops will figure out who he is and be down here beating the bushes for his wife and friends. We need to put distance between ourselves and Long Beach, and the same goes for Teddy and Catherine. I want us to pack up tonight and in the morning drive both cars to Teddy's apartment in Chicago. I have bank paper that needs his special talents, and I want him to sell the Packard. After that, you and I will head east in the Buick."

"But what about our new house in Nevada?" Verna's voice cracked with disappointment.

"Don't give up on me, old girl. The way things are, we need to spend a year to establish a legitimate business and identities to match. The little states north of New York are fresh territory for me and Teddy so it should be easy for us to blend in. When things die down, you and I will retire and make a safe move to Nevada. One way or the other, I plan to take your pretty picture in front of that damn big dam they're building, and sooner instead of later."

Verna came around to the back of the chair and gave Ed a little hug. He grunted "Ow," but she did not let go right away.

❧

Chapter Twenty Four

August 20, 1933

Verna was up and doing by 8 a.m. Sunday morning. Ed joined her an hour later, moving slowly, but moving. He washed the Packard inside and out and inspected every nook and cranny of the convertible for papers or debris that could connect the vehicle to him. He did not bother to give the Buick the same treatment, as he intended to keep the big black sedan. Except for the clothes Ed would wear that day, his shaving kit and his thirty-eight, Verna had completely packed all of his personal items the night before. Bentz placed his luggage and Verna's bags in the trunk of the Buick. Into the big back seat he placed his golf clubs and several boxes of books.

Next Bentz rolled and tied the seven railroad bonds stolen from People's Bank and placed them inside one of Verna's clean half-gallon Mason jars. He gently tightened the tin screw-on lid. Ed scrounged around in the cellar until he found some tongue and groove floorboards that had been left over from construction of the house. From those boards Bentz fashioned a homemade crate. He placed some rags inside the crate for padding, added a block of Verna's sealing wax, and then the Mason jar filled with bonds. Ed ran out of nails to close up the crate, so he placed the unfinished container in a feed sack which he tied shut with a piece of wire. The sack went into the trunk of the Buick next to the luggage. He would finish the crate later.

Verna fed them both bacon and eggs and black coffee. She made bacon and tomato sandwiches and put two in the front seat of the Packard for Ed and one in the Buick for her. While she did the dishes, Ed made his final reconnoiter of the cottage.

By the time he was finished it was almost noon, and Verna was ready to leave.

"Let's stop at Helen and Lester's place on the way out," she said, "because I told Helen I would come by at noon with a cherry pie." They drove both cars up the hill to the road and then motored down to the Gillis cottage. Verna walked down the driveway to the back door and tried the latch, but to her surprise it was locked. She set the pie on the stoop and knocked. No answer. She knocked again. Still no answer.

Verna walked round to the front porch and tried that door. It was also locked. She peered inside but could not see much because the interior was dark. Perplexed, she picked up the pie and walked back up the road where Ed was sitting in the Packard with the motor running.

"How strange! I'm positive I told Helen I would be by at noon to say goodbye before leaving town. She told me she would make a fresh pot of coffee to go with the pie."

"Maybe something came up," Ed offered. "Maybe she took Hazel into town to hunt up a lawyer for Earl. Anyway, we need to make tracks if we're going to reach Teddy's apartment before he and Catherine leave for supper." With that he turned the Packard around and waited by the side of the road while Verna returned to the Buick, started the motor and fell in behind. They then headed their two car caravan for Chicago.

It took Ed and Verna just under two hours to find Teddy's apartment building. It was located in the southeast corner of the intersection of Luella Avenue and 79th Street. Not having been there before, Ed had only the address to go on: 7095 South Luella. In the grid of Chicago proper, the avenues ran north and south and the streets east and west. Teddy had told Ed that Luella was about a dozen blocks west of Stony Island Avenue, which was a major north-south thoroughfare, so with that point of reference it was not difficult to find the correct intersection.

7095 South Luella was a three story high brick shoe box of a building, with the street side facades faced in decorative yellow brick and limestone ornamentation. The short side of the building faced 79th and the long side of the building ran down

Luella. A pharmacy was on the ground floor facing 79th. The rest of the building appeared to be residences, with a common door on the ground floor of the long side.

The Bentzs parked their cars at the curb and Ed got out to stretch. Verna quickly joined him.

"My back is still killing me," Ed complained, "so I'll duck into the drug store before we surprise Ted and Catherine." The big man held the door open for his petite wife and in they went.

Ed introduced himself and Verna as "Mr. and Mrs. Vaughner" and proceeded to order a bottle of aspirin and a tube of Ben-Gay analgesic ointment. He asked the pharmacist if he knew which apartment was being used by Ted and Catherine Craig. The druggist replied that the "nice young couple" was renting the first floor apartment in the rear of the building, although he had not seen either of them since Ted had come into the shop on Friday afternoon looking for a medicine to remedy Catherine's daily nausea.

"I don't think your friend Ted had put two and two together yet!" said the druggist as he winked at Verna.

"Well, yes, our friend Ted can be a little slow on the draw sometimes," Ed confessed. He paid for the medicines and escorted Verna out the door and around to the common entrance for the apartments. They entered and walked down a short hall to the last door. Ed knocked three times, and from inside they could hear Catherine call out, "One second, I'll be right there."

A moment later the door swung open to present Catherine in a blue Chinese silk dressing gown and heeled slippers. She took one look at Ed, let out a little shriek, and collapsed backwards onto a well worn armchair.

It took almost an hour for Catherine to sob and sniffle her way through the explanation of why Teddy was not at home. Just before noon, Lester Gillis had appeared unexpectedly on their doorstep. He apologized for being the bearer of bad tidings. The Grand Haven job had been a bust. Freddie drove off and left the troupe high and dry. A gunfight ensued during which every one of the bandits except Lester had been killed or captured. Gillis told the shaken Teddy that Ed had been shot at least twice in the back and had fallen to the street unconscious. Lester said he ran for his life empty-handed, stole a parked car, and against all odds made his way back to Long Beach. Now Gillis intended to "even the score" with that cur Freddie. Would Ted help?

"Teddy went into the bedroom and cried like a baby for ten minutes," said Catherine. "Finally," she continued, "Ted came back out all serious-like, with his hat in his hand, and told Lester to 'count me in'. Teddy called Freddie's mother's house and, sure enough, the bastard was with her for Sunday afternoon dinner!"

Verna handed Catherine a hankie so she could blow her nose. Catherine continued.

"Teddy was cool as a cucumber, even joked with Freddie, and never let on that Lester was here or that he knew that Freddie had deserted you. He told Freddie he wanted to talk about setting up a fence's shop in Chicago. Ted told Freddie to meet him at 7 p.m. at the south end of Soldier Field. Then Ted

and Lester left together. Lester said he needed to see a friend

about buying a 'throw-away gun' and some bullets."

Ed looked at his watch. It was almost 6:30.

"Catherine, do cabs come by this corner?" She said they

did. Bentz walked to the door and asked Verna to help him bring

in the bags. Once outside, he motioned for her to get inside the

Packard with him.

He reached into the glove box for his thirty-eight and

dropped it into his jacket pocket, saying, "Lester is off his rocker.

He will kill Freddie for sure, and he may decide to kill my brother

before Ted figures out that Lester's cock-n-bull story is a lie. I'm

taking a cab to Soldier Field. You stay here with Catherine. If

I'm not back with Ted by breakfast, you girls head for your

mother's house in Milwaukee."

Verna kissed Ed and whispered, "Please be careful,

darling, I'm too young to be a widow!"

❃

Chapter Twenty Five

August 20, 1933

An intermittent rain was starting to drizzle down the Yellow Cab's windshield as the driver turned east from Michigan Avenue toward the 18th Street pedestrian bridge. His lone passenger, a large fellow in a trench coat and brown fedora, pulled himself gingerly from the back seat and paid the fare and a generous tip. With a "Thanks, mister," the cabbie was off like a shot in search of another customer.

After bending at the waist several times to loosen his stiff back, Ed Bentz faced into the wind and set off across the bridge toward the 18th Street entrance of the World's Fair. The pedestrian walkway crossed over the wide expanse of the Illinois Central rail yard and ended at a ticket booth and gate. Ed paid his fifty cents admission, picked up a visitor's guide, and pushed through the turnstile. He took a moment to orient himself, then turned north toward Soldier Field.

The rain was steady now so Bentz turned up the collar of his coat and pulled down the brim of his hat. Twilight came quicker in the rain, and in response the Fair grounds were ablaze in lights. The most prominent structure was the Sky Ride. Each cable car was outlined in tubes of bright neon gas. Both towers, and the guy wires that stretched earthward from the top of each, were dotted with thousands of multi-colored bulbs. At the very top of each tower was an array of searchlights that projected both into the heavens and down toward the ground. The eerie sounds made by the tram engines and the steam jetting from the rear of the cable cars, combined with the haphazard twinkling of so many lights, transformed the Sky Ride into a gigantic nocturnal beast.

Bentz gritted his teeth in pain as he marched briskly past the Japanese and Chinese pavilions on his way to the south end of Soldier Field. His sore back complained at every step. Up ahead he could see that dozens of tourists were trying to stay dry by huddling under the scant cover provided by the overhang of the football stadium. In contrast, a short man was standing face full to the wind as he paced back and forth in the rain while staring up at the west tower. It was Lester, soaked to the bone. His soggy sports coat hung on him like wet paper.

When Gillis finally noticed Bentz the two were only a few paces apart. Lester immediately fumbled inside his coat for a gun, but Ed's thirty-eight was already out and pointed at Lester's mid-section.

"Relax, asshole, if I wanted you dead it would be over already," Bentz said in a low voice. "Where's my brother?"

"Up there," Gillis replied as he pointed to the west tower. "When Freddie saw I was with Ted, the rat bolted for the tower. Your brother ran after him. Freddie reached the elevator before Teddy. I've been waiting for both of them to come down, but no luck yet. Maybe they rode to the other side. I don't know."

Bentz said, "Give me your gun," and Gillis did as ordered. It was a Smith & Wesson K-22. Ed emptied the cylinder and pocketed the five rounds.

"I'm going up to look for Ted. If he comes back down before I do, tell him to go home."

"I can do that, Big Ed."

Bentz dropped Lester's revolver into a pocket, rubbed the small of his back with his free hand, and gazed up at the brightly shining steel giant. He started toward the base of the tower, then stopped to turn back and make eye contact with Gillis. With great deliberation Ed said, "Lester, if I see you again after tonight, I will kill you on sight."

As Ed approached the Sky Ride, he nonchalantly dropped Lester's empty handgun in a garbage bin and moved his own revolver to an inside pocket of the trench coat. The pocket had a flap that Bentz buttoned tight. Even to a trained eye there was no trace of a firearm on Bentz's person.

After joining the line of waiting customers, Ed realized that he had a choice to make: ride halfway up to the cable-car level, or take the express elevator to the observation decks. He decided to ride to the top, and if Teddy was nowhere to be found then descend and wait for him on the ground.

The elevator to the observation decks was the fastest made by Otis, and Ed left his throat in his shoes when the crowded car shot up sixty-two stories in under a minute. The elevator discharged its passengers to the enclosed lower deck, which was overcrowded because few souls were willing to brave the elements on the open upper deck during a summer storm. Ed traversed the lower deck twice before deciding that Ted was not part of the multitude. So he pushed his way through to the stairwell and deliberately climbed the single flight of stairs up to the top deck.

The weather was miserable. The wind had picked up and the rain drops stung Ed's face and neck as he slowly turned in a circle looking for Ted. Searchlights on top of the elevator engine room were blazing and filled the air with the smell of ozone, but the pedestrian deck was not particularly well lit. The east half of the deck was mostly covered in deep shadow.

The steel floor was finished with a mixture of battleship grey enamel and sand, but still the rain made walking about a bit dicey. Bentz edged slowly to the perimeter fence so that he could steady himself with one hand on the rail. He turned his back to the wind and peered out at the city's skyline and downward at the outline of Soldier Field. On a bright day or a clear night it would have been a marvelous view, but through the dark clouds of a rain storm everything just appeared cold and small. As Ed reached inside his coat for a cigar, a raspy voice from behind whispered, "Hello, Teddy."

Ed's bruised back made him slouch slightly as he turned toward the phantom speaker, and that probably saved his life. A knife came flashing down at Bentz's neck but missed, piercing instead the left shoulder epaulet of Ed's trench coat and becoming twisted in the fabric. Bentz frantically reached over his left shoulder with his right arm and managed to grab his assailant's knife hand. At the same time he pivoted into the attacker and grabbed for the other man's throat with his left hand. At the end of Ed's outstretched arm was a struggling Freddie Monahan, eyes bulging and nostrils flaring.

The two men grappled in desperation, Bentz trying to keep from being stabbed and Monahan gasping for air. Ed's feet started to slide out from under him on the wet deck, and Freddie took advantage. Freddie lunged forward with all his strength and Ed was slammed backward into a steel pedestal that supported a pair of observation binoculars. The post dug into Ed's back and the resulting pain made the big man cry out. Bentz was slowly forced to one knee but would not let go of Monahan's left hand. Freddie was above Ed now, repeatedly punching Ed in the side of the head with his crippled right hand while trying to twist his knife hand free for a second plunge. Bentz suddenly let go of Monahan's throat and gave the skinny man a quick punch in the solar plexus. Freddie gasped and spit but did not stop pummeling Ed with his right fist. Both men breathed heavily while Freddie slowly gained the advantage over his wounded opponent. Ed was bleeding from his left ear and fatigue started to make him wobble, so Freddie decided it was time to put the big fellow on his back. Almost spent, Ed watched helplessly as Freddie raised a size thirteen brogue in order to bring it crashing down on Ed's kneecap.

The blow never came. Instead, in the blink of an eye, Freddie was propelled up and over the handrail and out into the dark nothingness. Freddie started to scream but went suddenly quiet when his head slammed into a guy wire, leaving his limp body to free fall in silence.

Ed, exhausted and his head ringing, collapsed heavily in a puddle. Peering up through a veil of rain and sweat Ed thought he could make out his brother's goofy smile.

Teddy grasped Ed's hand and asked, "Hey, Big Brother, did you miss me?"

❧

Chapter Twenty Six

August 25, 1933

Ed and Verna spent several days with Teddy and Catherine so that Ed could nurse his back, Teddy could sell the Packard, and Verna could have the dry cleaner mend and clean Ed's trench coat. They did not return to Sleepy Nest but instead stopped at the dune top clubhouse of the Long Beach Country Club for a last meal before starting the long drive to Portland. Due to his custom of generous tipping, Ed was a favorite of the club's pro, Chip Godfrey. The pro cheerfully accepted Ed's invitation to join the Bentzs for a sandwich and cold drink in the Nineteenth Hole.

"Haven't seen you on the course for a week or so, Mr. Bentz. Have you been ill?" Godfrey inquired.

"Back went out on me, Chippy. Verna made me take it easy for a few days. Then a limb blew down on the top of the Packard, so I drove into Chicago to have the top repaired. Verna needed to shop so we spent several nights in the city."

"Are you staying with us past Labor Day?"

"Afraid not. I have pressing business in Memphis and Tucson, so Verna and I are boarding a westbound train tomorrow. Going to spend the winter in Mexico."

Verna chimed in. "Teddy and Catherine are going to join us. They were married in Mexico, you know."

"But we'll be back next year by Memorial Day." Bentz peered down the hill at the children frolicking around the club's Olympic-sized outdoor pool. "By the way, Chip, while we were gone did anyone come by the club looking for me? I have a new customer in Grand Rapids who thought he might join me for a round."

"No, Mr. Bentz, since the member-guest last month it's been just the usual faces. I've worked every day for the last two weeks, and I don't remember anybody stopping in the pro shop asking for you."

Verna headed to the ladies' while Ed walked over to the pro shop and paid double for a box of balls. He shook hands with Chip and headed for the door. The staff lined up outside to wave goodbye as the parking attendant pulled up with Ed's big Buick and opened the passenger door for Verna.

As the Bentzs breezed down the hill they passed by the Long Beach town hall and police station. In his rear view mirror Ed could see a dusty Maxwell with Michigan plates parked in the lot. The driver, a barrel-chested character in grey tweed trousers and a white shirt, was walking briskly toward the front door of the station. The man turned to peer at the big Buick for an instant before it rounded a curve and disappeared.

Ed steered his sedan across Highway 12 and drove south past the Pottawottomie Country Club. He crossed an overgrown creek and the Interurban track before rolling to a stop near a small bridge and tunnel that cut through the rising roadbed of the Grand Trunk. The tunnel harbored a sharp right turn, so only one car at a time could navigate the passage. A mile marker protruded upward from the blanket of crushed limestone that covered the top and sides of the track. Beneath the mile marker, surrounded by tall brambles, was the remainder of an old sycamore tree. It had been cleaved from top to bottom by lightening, and what remained was starting to rot.

Ed opened the trunk and removed the feed sack that contained the unfinished crate, the Mason jar filled with railroad bonds, and the block of sealing wax. He also retrieved a claw hammer, small sack of nails, and a garden spade. Bentz opened the hood, placed the can on the hot engine block, and dropped the wax into the can. The wax immediately began to melt into a clear ooze.

Verna watched her husband's machinations with amusement. "Say, Blackbeard, just what do you intend to do with our treasure?"

"Well, me lady, it be too 'hot' for the likes of Teddy right now." Ed's pirate voice made Verna roll her eyes, so he switched to the modern vernacular. "You and I need to lay low in Portland for at least a year. When it's safe to make our move to Nevada, we'll stop here on the way and dig up these little beauties for a grubstake." He used a handkerchief to insulate his fingers as he removed the can of liquid wax from the top of the hot car motor.

"In that case, add this to our booty, for good luck!" She unhooked the gold chain and Double Eagle from around her neck and handed it to her husband. He kissed her, unscrewed the lid, and dropped the necklace in the Mason jar next to the bonds. After screwing the lid on until it was tight, Ed dunked the top of the jar with great care into the molten wax to make a waterproof seal. He placed the jar in the crate and closed it up with several nails, then hoisted the box onto his left shoulder. Verna swung the garden spade over her right shoulder, slipped her arm

through Ed's, and the two made their way through the tall grass

to bury their loot.

✿

Epilogue

Earl Doyle, the only crook who was captured during the robbery of People's Bank, served fourteen years before being paroled in 1948. During his time behind bars Doyle steadfastly declined to name the other robbers of the bank.

George "Machine Gun" Kelly was arrested by Memphis Police and Bureau of Investigation agents on September 26, 1933. Convicted of kidnapping and given a life sentence, he spent seventeen years at Alcatraz and four years at Leavenworth before dying of a heart attack in prison in 1954.

Charles "Chuck" Fisher was arrested in December 1933 by a combined force of local police and Bureau agents. Fisher was turned over to the Bureau who saw to it that he was tried and convicted for a series of post office robberies. He was incarcerated at Leavenworth until the end of 1942. He never admitted complicity in the hold-up of People's Bank.

Clyde Barrow and Bonnie Parker were killed by ambush on a country road in Bienville Parish, Louisiana on the morning of May 23, 1934. Tom Hamer's men used Clyde's favorite weapon, the BAR, to riddle Barrow's Ford with more than one hundred fifty bullets.

Thomas "Tommy" Caroll (aka Thomas Murray) was mortally wounded in a shootout with local detectives in Waterloo, Iowa on June 7, 1934. He survived for seven hours in the hospital but refused to answer any questions other than to admit his identity.

John Dillinger was gunned down by Bureau of Investigation agents as he exited the Biograph Theater in Chicago on the evening of July 23, 1934. Melvin Purvis was the special agent in charge of the ambush.

Theodore "Teddy" Bentz served twenty-one years of a life sentence at the Michigan state prisons in Marquette and Jackson. While incarcerated he became a jailhouse lawyer on his own behalf, filing several motions for new trial (denied), leave for appeal to the Michigan Supreme Court (denied), and at least one habeas petition at the federal level (denied). Teddy was unable to charm the parole board, which periodically denied his requests for early release. In the 1950s, Grand Haven resident Claude Ver Duin became convinced of Teddy's innocence, and in 1955 Ver Duin approached Governor G. Mennen "Soapy" Williams about the possibility of a pardon for Bentz. The governor was never forced to decide the question of Teddy's pardon, because the parole board ordered Bentz' release in November 1955. Until the day he died, Teddy professed his innocence of the Grand Haven bank job.

On the afternoon of October 22, 1934, Charles "Pretty Boy" Floyd was mortally wounded at East Liverpool, Ohio in a shootout with a posse of G-Men and local police led by Melvin Purvis. It was reported that when Purvis tried to question the dying Floyd about his involvement in the Kansas City Massacre, Floyd replied, "Fuck you," and expired.

Lester "Baby Face Nelson" Gillis was an experienced, psychopathic killer by the time he joined forces with John Dillinger in March of 1934. In April of that year the partners-in-crime barely escaped a wild shootout with Bureau agents, led by Melvin Purvis, at the Little Bohemia lodge in northern Wisconsin. Gillis was killed in the Chicago suburb of Barrington during a running gun battle with Hoover's men on November 27, 1934. During the fight Gillis killed Herman Hollis, one of the federals who had hunted down "Pretty Boy" Floyd a month earlier.

Helen Gillis was captured soon after her husband's death. She served a year in jail for violating a previous probation, and upon her release was immediately arraigned in federal court for "harboring" Lester. She pleaded guilty. Ronnie and Darlene grew to adulthood, married and moved to other cities but managed to stay close to their mother. Helen never remarried.

Helen died in 1987 from a cerebral hemorrhage, and, as she wished, was buried next to Lester in the Gillis family plot.

Melvin Purvis retired from the Bureau in 1935 and entered law practice. He died from a self-inflicted gunshot wound in 1960. Legend has it that Purvis shot himself with one of the forty-five caliber pistols that had been used to kill Dillinger.

The FBI caught up to Alvin "Creepy" Karpis in New Orleans on May 1, 1936. J. Edgar Hoover flew down from Washington so that he could be personally present at the capture of the last "public enemy" on the Bureau's famous list. Karpis was imprisoned at Alcatraz, where he eventually held the record for the longest incarceration at the Rock. Paroled in 1969, he committed suicide in 1979.

Lawrence DeWitt retired from the Grand Haven Police Department in 1955. He had been on the force for thirty-four years, twenty-three of them as chief of police. During retirement he served a stint as justice of the peace. In 1983 DeWitt passed away at the age of ninety-three. He was buried in Grand Haven, the town he served and protected for four decades.

Verna Bentz left Portland in haste at the end of July, 1934. She and Ed were reunited in New York City for a short time. While they were on the run, Verna became pregnant with their only child, a daughter, who was born in the fall of 1935. By the time Ed Bentz was finally hunted down and captured by the FBI in 1936, Verna was back in Milwaukee. The FBI must have been keeping Verna under surveillance in hope of catching Ed, because as soon as he was arrested in Brooklyn, she was arrested in Milwaukee and charged with "harboring" her husband. That turn of events gave Ed extra incentive to plead guilty to the Danville bank robbery. This writer believes Verna passed away before 1953.

Edward Wilhelm Bentz was arrested in Brooklyn by federal agents on March 13, 1936. He pled guilty to the Danville bank robbery but refused to name his accomplices. At sentencing Ed asked to be incarcerated at Alcatraz because, times being what they were, "All my friends are there." The system obliged him. He began his twenty year sentence at the federal penitentiary in Atlanta and after two months was moved to Alcatraz. Bentz was paroled from Alcatraz in 1948, but was immediately transported to Massachusetts to stand trial on an outstanding larceny charge. Once again the old yegg pled guilty and refused to name names. After Massachusetts released Bentz in 1953, he went to live with his daughter Jeannette in Chicago. Ed quickly fell into debt, due in part to the expensive gifts he lavished on his daughter. In 1954 he held up a feed store near Green Bay and was captured within a few days. Ed did eight years in a Wisconsin prison for that crime. When Wisconsin released Bentz, he was sent back to federal incarceration for a year because the Wisconsin conviction constituted a violation of his federal parole. Finally, at age sixty-nine, and after he had served almost thirty years in a series of prisons, Ed Bentz was a free man. He returned to Tacoma and lived quietly near a brother and sister. The man who J. Edgar Hoover proclaimed "King of the Bank Robbers" died of a heart attack on October 31, 1979, at the age of eighty-five.

"Freddie" Monahan was probably an alias used by a novice criminal whom Lester Gillis knew from The Patch. Freddie's body, and for that matter the railroad bonds stolen from People's Bank, have never been recovered.

Finis

Acknowledgments

—

The author received gracious and enthusiastic assistance from many friends, old and new, in the preparation of this historical novel. Special thanks to Jeanette Weiden, Loutit District Library; Sue Kennedy, Ottawa County Circuit Court; Lisa Ashcraft, JP Morgan Chase; Capt. Rick Yonker, Grand Haven Department of Public Safety; Gary Rosema, Ottawa County Sheriff; Denny Dryer, Dryer Architectural Group; Wallace Ewing of the Tri-Cities Historical Museum; James Beukema, past Grand Haven Township Supervisor; Sara Eagin; Joanne Crater, Hudson

Public Library; Don and Mary Ann Klein; Barbara Bonema;

David and Dottie Seibold; Phil and Jane King; and to my best

friend, Laura.

HG

Glossary

Creeper - a bank robber who pretends to be a customer and sneaks into an open vault when the bank's employees are preoccupied with other customers.

Get - the detailed driving directions for the escape route.

Interurban - a generic term for an electric commuter train. The South Shore Line still operates such a train between Michigan City and Chicago.

Jug - the type of vault and/or safe inside the target bank.

Klootzak - Flemish for "fool".

Mark - the bank to be robbed.

The Patch - Chicago's "Little Italy", settled originally by Sicilian immigrants. Today the neighborhood is referred to as Smith Park.

Rank - inquisitive bystanders lining up on the sidewalk.

Yegg - a safecracker; a thief who uses special tools or explosives to open a vault during the wee hours.

Bibliography

The information used by the author in the preparation of this story was gleaned from many sources, including conversations with the two characters still living, descendants of some of the characters, or decedents of persons who knew the characters. Regarding written and documentary materials, what the author found most useful are listed below:

Books

B. Burrough, *Public Enemies, America's Greatest Crime Wave and the Birth of the FBI, 1933-34*, Penguin Books (2004).

Ewing & Seibold, *The Grand Haven Area 1905-1975 in Vintage Postcards*, Arcadia Publishing (2003).

S. Gleisten, *Chicago's 1933-34 World's Fair: A Century of Progress in Vintage Postcards*, Arcadia Publishing (2002).

Helmer & Mattix, *The Complete Public Enemy Almanac*, Cumberland House Publishing, Inc. (2007).

J. Edgar Hoover, *Persons in Hiding*, Little, Brown and Company (1938).

L. Lohr, *Fair Management: The Story of a Century of Progress, A Guide For Future Fairs*, The Cuneo Press, Inc. (1952).

E.R. Milner, *The Lives and Times of Bonnie and Clyde*, Southern Illinois University Press (1996).

Nickel & Helmer, *Baby Face Nelson - Portrait of a Public Enemy*, Cumberland House (2002).

Rydell, Findling & Pelle, *Fair America - World's Fairs in the United States*, Smithsonian Institution Press (2000).

David H. Seibold, D.D.S., *Grand Haven - In the Path of Destiny*, Great Lakes Printing Solutions (2007).

J. Schuler & H. Schuler, *Schuler's - Fresh Recipes and Warm Memories*, Huron River Press (2004).

B. Stodola, *Images of America - Michigan City Beach Communities - Sheridan, Long Beach, Duneland, Michigan Shores*, Arcadia Publishing (2003).

B. Yenne, *Tommy Gun - How General Thompson's Submachine Gun Wrote History*, St. Martin's Press (2009).

Newspapers

The Beacher (weekly newspaper; Michigan City, IN), "Sands of Time - Duneland Stories", July 17, 2003.

The Grand Haven Daily Tribune: August 18, 1933; August 19, 1933; August 22, 1933; August 24, 1933; August 25, 1933; September

6, 1933; September 12, 1933; September 26, 1933; May 23, 1934; June 8, 1934; July 22, 1934; October 22, 1934; October 23, 1934; April 26, 1980 (Peoples Bank grand re-opening supplement); August 13, 2003.

Hudson Post Gazette, August 22, 1933.

The Ludington Dailey News, April 13, 1936.

The Muskegon Chronicle: August 18, 1933; August 19, 1933; August 21, 1933; August 23, 1933; August 24, 1933; August 25, 1933
.

The Nashville Banner, August 3, 1933; August 4, 1933; August 7, 1933 (all special reports by visitor Lera Knox).

The Seattle Dailey Times, March 13, 1936; March 14, 1936; March 16, 1936.

The Springfield Union, May 22, 1954.

Trenton Evening Times, March 13, 1936.

Articles

M. Amundson, "Eddie Bentz", *Columbia - The Magazine of Northwest History*, Vol. 23 No. 2 (Summer 2009).

E, Bentz, "I, Edward Bentz, depose and say . . ." , *Argosy* (January 1951).

J. Chiles, "Age-old battle to keep safes safe from 'creepers, soup men and yeggs'", *Smithsonian* (July 1984).

R. Meima, "A forgotten city", *Michigan History Magazine*, pp 397-409 (Volume V, July-October 1921).

Other

Ottawa County (Michigan) Circuit Court file 2849 for *People v Theodore Bentz*, originally opened in 1934 and now stored in the old gypsum mine beneath Grand Rapids, Michigan.

Felony file for August 18, 1933 People's Bank robbery, maintained as a historical record by the Grand Haven Department of Public Safety.

Assorted photographs retained by JP Morgan Chase for it's Grand Haven branch at Washington and Third Streets, fka People's Savings Bank.

W. Ewing, *(i) Directory – People -- Northwest Ottawa County, (ii) Directory – Buildings and Sites – Northwest Ottawa County, (iii) Directory – Businesses, Industries and Other Organizations – Northwest Ottawa County 1808-1975* (Seventh Printing, Revised Ed., June 2008).

FBI File no. 7-115, *George "Machine Gun" Kelly Summary*.

FBI File no. 7-576, Section no. 241, *Barker-Karpis Gang Summary*.

FBI File no. 26-4114, *Bonnie and Clyde*.

FBI File no. 62-28915, Section no. 58, Serials 2381-2426, *Charles "Pretty Boy" Floyd, Kansas City Massacre*.

FBI File no. 62-29777-1, Section no. 1, Serials 1-28, *John Dillinger*.

FBI File no. 91-57. On an Internet site maintained by the FBI for the general public, the Bureau describes this file as pertaining to "Baby Face Nelson's involvement in the 1934 robbery of the People's Savings Bank in Grand Haven, Michigan". In addition to getting the year wrong, the Bureau mis-characterizes the content of the file. It is, in truth, filled with correspondence and other items that Theodore Bentz showered upon the FBI between 1937 and 1951 in his efforts obtain a new trial. The contents of the file have very little to do with Lester Gillis.

Audio interview of Art Welling taken on August 20, 1973. This recording is part of the oral history archives for Grand Haven, MI maintained by the Loutit District Library.

Official Guidebook of the World's Fair of 1934, published by A Century of Progress International Exposition, Chicago, The Cuneo Press, Inc. (1934).

A Century of Progress - The 1933-34 World's Fair, The University of Chicago Library, Digital Activities & Collections (http://century.lib.uchicago.edu).

Large scale aerial photographs of the development of Northerly Island, and of the 1933 Century of Progress, maintained as wall displays inside the old terminal building of Meigs Field, Chicago.